A Marriage Made in Italy
The Wedding Planning Guide
(2006 – 2008)

Callie Copeman-Bryant

All rights reserved. No part of the work 'A Marriage Made in Italy' may be lent, re-sold, hired or otherwise circulated, reproduced, stored in a retrieval system or transmitted on any form or by any means, electronic, mechanical, photocopying, recording, scanning or otherwise. Written permission to make a copy or copies must be obtained by the author in advance.

The right of Callie Copeman-Bryant to be identified as the author of this work has been asserted by her in accordance with the Copyright, Designs & Patents Act 1988.

Copyright © Callie Copeman-Bryant 2006

A Marriage Made Publications
www.amarriagemade.co.uk

First published 2006

ISBN: 978-1-84728-657-4

A Marriage Made and the A Marriage Made logo are trademarks.

A Marriage Made books provide independent advice and the author does not accept advertising in guide books or payment in exchange for listing or endorsing any business, or for providing positive coverage. All statements and opinions regarding businesses and locations are subjective.

The material contained herein is set out in good faith for general guidance, but no warranty can be made about the accuracy or completeness of its content. The author cannot be responsible for any errors within this work, or accept any responsibility or liability for any loss or expense incurred, or consequences arising as a result of relying on particular circumstances or statements made. Laws and regulations are complex and liable to change, and currency rates change regularly, so it is vital that readers should check the relevant legal, financial and logistical details for themselves. Details such as addresses, telephone numbers, website and email addresses are also liable to change.

Contents

Introduction – Getting Married Abroad........................ 2

Why Italy?........................ 5

Legal Requirements............. 8
   UK Legal Requirements........ 9
   Irish Legal Requirements..... 11
   US Legal Requirements....... 12
   Affidavit of Single Status...... 13
   Presentation of Documents... 13
   Consular Districts............... 14
   Marriage Certificates & Registration...................... 14

Planners or DIY?.................. 15
   Tour Operators................... 17
   Wedding Co-ordinators........ 22
   "Do it Yourself"................... 25

Types of Ceremony............... 26
   Civil Ceremonies................. 26
   Catholic Ceremonies........... 29
   Protestant, Jewish & Other Religious Ceremonies.......... 30
   Symbolic & Renewal of Vow Ceremonies....................... 31
   Same Sex Partnerships........ 31

Customs, Traditions & Etiquette............................ 32
   Italian Traditions................ 33
   Italian Superstitions............ 34
   Major Differences............... 35
   Invitations....................... 37
   Wedding Information Websites.......................... 40
   Gifts.............................. 41

Apparel........................... 43
   Transportation & Logistics.. 43
   Keeping Cool................... 45
   Suit Hire........................ 46

Task List & Planning Tools... 47
   Task List......................... 48
   Useful Planning Sites.......... 52

Budget Planner & Finances.. 53
   Budget Planner................. 53
   Exchange Rates................ 54
   Insurance....................... 55

Country Information........... 56
   Average Climate Conditions. 56
   Public Holidays................. 56

Glossary......................... 57
   Italian Sayings.................. 57
   English – Italian Wedding Dictionary....................... 58

Country-Wide Contacts........ 59
   Embassies & Consulates..... 60
   Marriage Offices............... 61
   Photographers.................. 62
   Wedding Co-ordinators........ 63
   Tour Operators................. 65

Bibliography & Resources... 66

Acknowledgements............ 67

Index............................ 68

Introduction: Getting Married Abroad

"When you get married in this part of the world your wedding will have a bigger wow-factor than any traditional UK wedding. Guaranteed."

Sorrento Bride

As soon as the boom in low-cost travel aligned itself with a change in European marriage laws, the sharp rise in European weddings became inevitable. After all, when you can fly to Rome for less than it costs to take the train from London to Edinburgh, the old arguments against weddings abroad tend fall by the wayside. Getting married abroad is still new enough to be unique, and that brings many advantages: you're certain to be embarking on unchartered territory, at least as far as your guests are concerned, an aspect which allows you to be as creative as you wish. You have *carte blanche* when it comes to style - for example you can choose whether to transport a traditional wedding to a beautiful location, have a country-themed wedding or just make your own rules: don't fancy a predictable, flower-lined limo to take you to your wedding in Ravello? Then hire a red Ferrari and whiz along the Amalfi Coast road with your veil streaming out behind you instead. Or pop on a white lid and a pair of sunnies, and buzz along to your wedding on a hired Vespa. There are no expectations, which leaves only the unexpected.

But of course this scope for a unique kind of wedding comes with a unique kind of planning. At some stage you'll doubtless flick through the pages of a traditional wedding planning book and realise that the legal information is somewhat lacking. You'll come across checklists and timelines in bridal magazines and find that, at least for you, only half the tasks are there. You'll visit wedding websites and search in vain for overseas reception venues, florists and hairdressers.

So here is a guide to help you, written by someone who did it the hard way. I got married on the Amalfi Coast in 2005, having had to overcome a shocking lack of information during the planning phase. If finding all the information in one place was too much to wish for, at least finding all the information *easily* ought to be attainable. It wasn't. Searching for hotels in an Italian town might be easy, but try googling for a hairdresser or a florist. In Italian. How could I find out if I still need to Give Notice? What vows would I be making to my husband? All pretty important things to know, I thought.

I became obsessive about finding the information, and when I'd finished I resolved to do something about the situation for other poor, confused couples. Research began on the first books in the series in late 2005. In preparation for the first research trips in 2006, hotels and restaurants were extensively researched to ensure that only companies with the best reviews and reputations were approached for inclusion - these hotel and venue reviews have been divided up into small, separate Area Guides to give you instant, user-friendly access to relevant advice rather than a tome of unnecessary information. All reviewed venues in the series have been personally visited and verified: of these, the companies featuring the "Top Pick" logo were felt to offer the very best in the area in terms of service, location and value for money, although do bear in mind that the guides feature just a selection of the venues available, and there are many other, excellent choices out there.

In this particular book you'll find task lists, recommendations, legal requirements and more, all tailored to the couple getting married in Italy, and all with the experience of someone who's been there and got the t-shirt. The book is predominantly written for UK couples, although information relevant to those of you from Ireland and the US has also been included. I hope you find it of some use; good luck and enjoy the planning!

A Marriage Made in Italy Area Guides

- The Italian Lakes
- Venice & The Veneto
- Marche
- Tuscany & Umbria
- Abruzzo
- Rome
- Puglia
- Capri & Ischia
- The Amalfi Coast
- Calabria

For more information on the Area Guides (and other country guides), visit the A Marriage Made website at www.amarriagemade.co.uk

Why Italy?

"We wanted to get married overseas, but didn't want a long haul destination. There were a few options, but Italy was by far the best."

Cortona Bride

Having picked up this book, you've either decided on Italy already or you're pretty close to making that decision. Either way, I'm going to be making a strong case for Italy, not just because there are some very good reasons why, after Cyprus, it's the most popular European wedding destination for UK couples; I'll be making a strong case for Italy because, frankly, *you're* going to need one. At least as soon as you can make yourself heard over the sound of dropping jaws when you announce to your family and friends that you're not getting married on home turf.

In all honesty, telling people you're getting married abroad is an experience in itself. Telling your family is hard enough - they'll look at you slack-jawed, wondering where you got such a hare-brained idea from, certain that you haven't actually put any real thought into this and coming up with a million reasons why it just isn't possible. Go easy on yourself and book the wedding in the school holidays if you have parents or teachers to invite, and make sure everyone realises that they can get there on a low-cost flight and that B&Bs aren't that expensive. Be ready with examples of accommodation options and costs to back up your argument and stymie any opposition. Nip the cynics in the bud. It's more than possible to do this and for everyone to enjoy it, and bear in mind that the biggest cynics now will probably be the ones who enjoy it the most on the day.

Telling colleagues and acquaintances is just plain irritating. Unless either you or your fiancé is Italian (in which case you're off the hook), they will all invariably ask "so why Italy?", as if to say "but what's wrong with Basildon High Street?" You will find yourself shrugging apologetically, while wondering why it is that the conversation you're having wouldn't be taking place if you'd said you were getting married in the Caribbean.

So aside from the kind of climate, culinary delights, hospitality and magnificent scenery that you're going to be hard-pushed to find at a Location Near You, here are some points in Italy's favour that will either help you make up your mind, or back up your case:

Accessibility

Almost all the major cities in Italy are well served by low-cost airlines from the UK. For those that aren't, the brilliant transport network makes the more isolated locations pretty easy to reach. Flying time is between two hours (London to Verona) and three hours (London to Brindisi), making it ideal for couples who are sensitive to their guests' ability to travel. In fact with an afternoon wedding, it's more than possible for a guest to arrive on the day of the ceremony, stay overnight and return the next day.

Cost

In 2005 a study published by Morgan Stanley found that the average guest paid £300 to attend a wedding in the UK, while a similar study by Halifax Travel showed that guests attending a wedding abroad spent around £1300. I'd certainly dispute the latter figure; it doesn't take much research to discover that, depending on your location and the time of year, a guest can attend a European wedding for an amount closer to that average UK figure. Of course with the range of options available it's difficult to state a definite amount – some of your guests may choose to spend a week in an expensive hotel, whilst others may spend two days in a bed and breakfast. In the spring of 2006 I travelled to Rome with a low-cost airline, stayed for two nights in a budget hotel and the entire trip cost me under £300. A similar trip to Sorrento cost under £200.

Communication

English is widely spoken and Italian isn't a difficult language to learn, so you'll successfully understand and be understood. In tourist areas like the Amalfi Coast, Venice and the Lake District, you'd be (unfortunately) forgiven for thinking English is the first language, whereas in some of the more rural areas you'll find things a little more challenging. A basic grasp of Italian in the latter case is essential; in the former, it is simply good manners. Either way, unlike in some other European countries, the inhabitants don't pretend not to understand your attempts at communication - in fact the Italians are charmed by any attempt to speak their language. Just learn the essentials, put the stereotypical stress on the second to last syllable, roll your "r"s and gesticulate wildly. It's rather therapeutic, and you'll find it pretty easy to get by.

Practicality

Italy has enviable residency requirements. Some tour operators and hotels impose their own minimum stay requirements, and if you're arranging things yourself you'll need to allow a few days to put all your paperwork in place when you get there, but legally you can leave it just about as late as you like to arrive in the country which gives it a distinct advantage over places like France (and indeed the UK) which have long residency requirements that can be difficult to work around.

Familiarity

The ceremony formats are similar enough to British, Irish and American weddings to feel familiar, but different enough to offer some interest for you and your guests. Civil ceremonies do differ in style to the format your guests will be used to but will be translated into English and are easy to follow, whereas religious weddings of course share the same format throughout the world. With regards to the reception you have the option to follow a variety of traditions or simply make up your own rules to fit your personal style.

Legality.
Provided you fulfil all the requirements, you can rest assured your marriage will be legally binding in the UK, Ireland and the US, and there isn't much more paperwork involved than there would be if you were getting married at home. That which *is* involved is relatively straightforward, although it is a distinct advantage to employ a co-ordinator to handle this aspect as it can become rather bureaucratic at times.

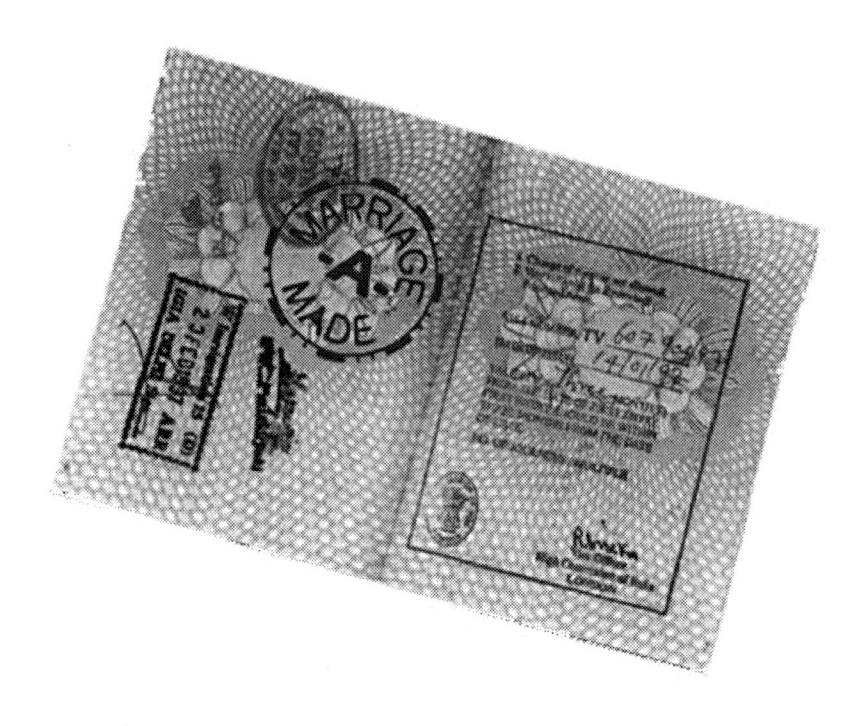

Legal Requirements

"In Italy where the legal requirements can be quite intricate, it's useful to employ a wedding planner who will know exactly what is needed."

www.weddings-abroad-guide.com

All you have to remember when you're planning your wedding in Italy is that you have two sets of legal requirements to fulfil. First of all your homeland legal requirements (which you'd have to fulfil regardless of where the marriage takes place), and secondly the legal requirements specific to marriages in Italy. All sets of legal requirements are outlined below, but the key is to check, double check and triple check everything with your co-ordinator if you have one, and with the relevant consulate offices to make sure everything is in place. When you talk to other couples planning their weddings at home they will tell you that their greatest fear is the dress not fitting, or the flowers not turning up. *Your* greatest fear is getting yourselves and your guests out to Italy and discovering that your paperwork is incomplete and the wedding can't take place. Bear all that in mind, double check the requirements and keep copies of everything. Apart from that, try to relax – the requirements mercifully aren't too complicated.

©JoAnne Dunn Photographer

Before you do anything, however, check with the relevant Italian Town Hall (*Comune*), Registry Office (*Anagrafe*) or your co-ordinator to establish when you need to submit your documentation. In some areas the Town Hall does not accept documents more than three months old, while in other areas (such as Rome) they won't secure your booking until they receive your *Nulla Osta*. Your first job is therefore to find out the requirements in your particular, chosen area. I'd list them here, but they are so varied and so subject to change that to do so may well be misleading and possibly even out of date by the time the information goes to print.

Legal Requirements for UK Citizens

Before a UK citizen marries in Italy, they must fulfil the same legal requirements that they would if they were marrying in the UK, and follow the same procedures for Giving Notice (although the time scales differ from the standard UK wedding procedure). These are the basic requirements that you need to fulfil to legally marry under UK law:

- Both parties must be over the age of 18, or have parental consent if aged between 16 and 18.
- Any previous marriage must have ended in bereavement or divorce.
- You must have been of the opposite sex to each other at birth.
- Certain degrees of relationship are forbidden. These are as follows:

A man may not marry his:	A woman may not marry her:
Mother	Father
Step-mother	Step-father
Mother-in-law	Father-in-law
Former mother-in-law	Former father-in-law
Adoptive mother	Adoptive father
Former adoptive mother	Former adoptive father
Daughter	Son
Step-daughter	Step-son
Former step-daughter	Former step-son
Daughter-in-law	Son-in-law
Former daughter-in-law	Former son-in-law
Adoptive daughter	Adoptive son
Former adoptive daughter	Former adoptive son
Sister	Brother
Half-sister	Half-brother
Grandmother	Grandfather
Step-grandmother	Step-grandfather
Grand-daughter	Grandson
Step-grand-daughter	Step-grandson
Grandson's wife	Grand-daughter's husband
Aunt	Uncle
Niece	Nephew
Great-grandmother	Great-grandfather
Great-grand-daughter	Great-grandson

Cousins: Although it is legal for cousins to marry it is advisable for them to consult a GP if they wish to have children, to ensure there are no genetic reasons why it would be inadvisable.

Step-relatives: Certain step-relatives can marry as long as they are both over 21 years of age, and as long as the younger member of the couple was not treated as a child of the older person's family, and did not live in the same household as the older person before the age of 18.

Relatives-in-law: A man may marry his sister-in-law, and a woman may marry her brother-in-law. However, in the case of all other relatives-in-law, marriage can only take place if both members of the couple are over the age of 21 and the family members creating the in-law relationship are deceased.

Where both parties are British Nationals domiciled in the UK, the process you need to follow is this:

- As soon as you have established the requirements of the local Italian Town Hall (*see page 8*), make an appointment to Give Notice at your local Registry Office. Both couples must Give Notice to a UK Superintending Registrar in the district in which they are resident. The process is the same as if you were marrying in the UK, but whereas with UK weddings you Give Notice as soon as you set your wedding date, in your case you will need to work according to the deadlines set by the Italian Town Hall (and then periodically check with the Italian Consulate or Wedding Planner in case the rules change at any time). When visiting the Superintending Registrar to Give Notice, you will each need to take the following documents:
  - Original or certified copies of your full (long) birth certificates
  - Passports
  - Evidence of the termination of any previous marriage (either a Death Certificate or Decree Absolute) along with the previous marriage certificate
  - If a name differs from that shown on the birth certificate, a copy of the relevant Deed Poll certificate
  - Consent of a parent or guardian if under 18
- Your Notice will be displayed for 16 days to ensure there are no objections to the marriage. After this time has passed, you can collect your Certificates of Authority

If only one of the parties is domiciled in the UK, the other party must post Notice of Marriage at the British Consulate in the district where they are resident.

If both parties are currently living in Italy, they must reside in the relevant Italian Consular district for 21 days immediately preceding the Giving of Notice at the British Consulate in the relevant district.

The following documents must then be presented to the relevant Italian Town Hall in order to produce the *Nulla Osta* (Certificate of No Impediment), which is crucial if the marriage is to take place. If you have a co-ordinator acting for you, they will present the following documents to the Town Hall on your behalf:

- The Certificates of Authority you collected from the Registry Office after Giving Notice
- Original or certified copies of your full (long) birth certificates
- Photocopies of passports

- Copies of two witnesses' passports, detailing addresses and occupations
- If a name differs from that shown on the birth certificate, a copy of the relevant Deed Poll certificate
- Copy of adoption certificate, if relevant
- Consent of a parent or guardian if under 18
- Evidence of the termination of any previous marriage (either a Death Certificate or Decree Absolute along with the previous marriage certificate). Note that a divorced woman who wishes to remarry in Italy may only do so after 300 days have passed from the date of Decree Absolute (dispensations can be applied for through a *Tribunale Civile* - for further information contact the *Ufficio Matromonio* of the Town Hall in the district the marriage is to take place).

******Please note that this information is given for general guidance only. Further information should be obtained from the British Embassy (www.britishembassy.gov.uk)******

Legal Requirements for Irish Citizens

Before an Irish citizen marries in Italy, they must fulfil the same legal requirements that they would if they were marrying in Ireland. The basic requirements are:

- Both parties must have the capacity to marry each other, must freely consent to the marriage and observe the necessary formalities as required by the laws of the State.
- Both parties must be over the age of 18, or have obtained the permission of the Circuit Family Court or High Court if under 18.
- Each person must give at least three months' written notification to the appropriate Registrar. The three months' notice does not commence until notification has been received.
- You must have been of the opposite sex to each other at birth.
- The marriage must not contravene the degrees of relationship that are forbidden under Irish law.

Contact the Consular Section of the Department of Foreign Affairs (or the nearest Irish Embassy, if living abroad) who will send you an application form and questionnaire which you need to complete in order to obtain your Certificate of Freedom to Marry (*Nulla Osta*). The documents need to be authorised by a solicitor or notary, and returned to the Department with a copy of your long birth certificate, certified copies of your passports and the fee (approx €20 in total). The Department will then forward this to the Irish Embassy in Rome, who in turn will forward it to your relevant Consular District. The Irish Embassy recommends applications to be made around four months before the date of the wedding, and you should receive your *Nulla Osta* around a month before the wedding.

The documents you need to produce are:
- Original birth certificates
- Certified copies of passports
- Completed Questionnaire Form MP1
- Completed Statutory Declaration Form MP2 (or MP2B if divorced)
- Copies of two witnesses' passports, detailing addresses and occupations
- If a name differs from that shown on the birth certificate, a copy of the relevant Deed Poll certificate
- Copy of adoption certificate, if relevant
- Evidence of the termination of any previous marriage (either a death certificate along with the previous marriage certificate or, if divorced, the Final Decree along with the previous marriage certificate and original Petition of Divorce). Note that a divorced woman who wishes to remarry in Italy may only do so after 300 days have passed from the date of Final Decree (dispensations can be applied for through a *Tribunale Civile* - for further information contact the *Ufficio Matromonio* of the Town Hall in the district the marriage is to take place).
- A divorced foreign national wishing to marry an Irish Citizen must also complete Statutory Declaration Form MP2D and provide a copy of their Carta d'Identita.

*******Please note that this information is given for general guidance only. Further information should be obtained from The Irish Embassy (www.ambasciata-irlanda.it and http://foreignaffairs.gov.ie)******

Legal Requirements for US Citizens

Before a US citizen marries in Italy, they must fulfil the same legal requirements that they would if they were marrying in the US.

The documents that must be provided to obtain the *Nulla Osta* are:
- Copies of passports or Armed Forces ID Card
- Certified (Apostille sealed) translated copies of your birth certificates, showing the names of both parents
- Consent of a parent or guardian if under 18
- A declaration (*atto notorio*) sworn to by four witnesses, preferably before an Italian consular officer in the United States stating that, according to the laws to which the citizen is subject in the US, there is no obstacle to his or her marriage. If this cannot be done in the US before leaving for Italy, it may be done in Italy at a *Pretura*, or before a mayor or town clerk.
- Apostille sealed and translated evidence of the termination of any previous marriage (either a Death Certificate or Final Divorce or Annulment Decree along with the previous marriage certificate). Note that a divorced woman who wishes to remarry in Italy may only do so after 300 days have passed from the date of Final Decree (dispensations can be applied for through a *Tribunale Civile* - for further information

contact the *Ufficio Matromonio* of the Town Hall in the district the marriage is to take place).

These documents should be translated into Italian and the translation must be certified by an Italian Consular Officer.

******Please note that this information is given for general guidance only. Further information should be obtained from the US Embassy (www.usembassy.it)******

Affidavit of Single Status

Although many books and sites will tell you that you will need to provide an Affidavit of Single Status, the checks carried out by the UK Registry Office when you Give Notice cover this aspect and you shouldn't need any additional paperwork to support it. As always, however, check with your co-ordinator or the Town Hall; it would be unusual for them to specifically request an affidavit in addition to your Certificate of Authority, but if they do it's easy enough to arrange - simply contact a local solicitor and make an appointment for both of you to swear an affidavit. If the solicitor or Town Hall don't have specific wording for you to use, draw up your own letter along the following lines:

"My full name is <Name> and I reside at <Address>. My nationality is <Nationality>. My date of birth is <DOB>. My occupation is that of a <Occupation>. My passport number is <Passport Number>. I <Name> do declare that I am single/divorced/widowed and free of any bond of engagement or marriage and can lawfully enter into this, my first/second marriage."

The solicitor will require you to swear and sign this statement, before signing and stamping it themselves. The process should cost around £5 per letter.

Presentation of Documents

The above mentioned documents must be presented to the *Ufficiale di Stato Civile* (Civil Registrar) in the district in which you intend to marry at least two weeks before the proposed marriage date, although this does not need to be done in person if you have a co-ordinator or tour operator acting on your behalf. It will take around three to five working days to process the paperwork and produce your *Nulla Osta*. If one of you is Italian or resident in Italy, banns are posted in the *comune* (Town Hall) for two Sundays, and the wedding can take place four days after the second Sunday; for non Italians or non Italian residents, this requirement is waived.

Unless both of you are Italian, the law requires you to have an approved translator present at the ceremony, which is normally a service your co-ordinator will provide. The wedding must be performed by a local civil or religious official in a building owned and approved by the Catholic Church or Town Hall depending on your type of ceremony.

Consular Districts

There are four consular districts in Italy: Milan, Florence, Rome and Naples. With respect to the most popular wedding destinations in Italy, they cover the following areas:

Como	Milano (Milan)
Lake District	
Lecco	
Milan	
Padua	
Venice	
Verona	
Arezzo	Firenze (Florence)
Florence	
Lucca	
Pisa	
Siena	
Tuscany	
Umbria	
Rome	Roma (Rome)
Amalfi Coast	Napoli (Naples)
Amalfi	
Capri	
Ischia	
Positano	
Ravello	
Sorrento	

Marriage Certificates & Registration

After the marriage has taken place you will be issued with a Marriage Certificate which must be authenticated and presented to the local Consular Office (again, a process your co-ordinator or tour operator will take care of). Marriages that take place in Italy are recognised, but not registered, in the UK, Ireland or the US. Your Italian wedding certificate will be accepted as official proof of marriage back at home, although some companies may request an official translation. However, although the marriage will not be registered, it is a good idea to lodge a copy of your marriage certificate with the General Registrar Office (for UK couples) in case you lose your own copy, as it's far easier to obtain certified copies through the GRO than it is to apply for copies from the Town Halls in Italy. For this reason it is a good idea to request two copies of your marriage certificate from the Consular Office at the outset – one to send to the GRO, and one to keep. The GRO can be contacted at www.gro.gov.uk.

Planners or DIY?

"Don't make the mistake of thinking you're just planning a normal wedding in a distant location: the whole process has a tendency to evolve in ways you might not expect!"
Lake Garda Bride

Almost all weddings that take place in the UK are planned on what I call a DIY basis, usually by the bride with a little help from the groom, significantly more help from the family and often too much help from the prospective mother-in-law. Wedding co-ordinators tend to be viewed as an expensive luxury; after all, there are many wedding planning books, magazines and internet sites to help you understand the legal requirements if you don't know them already, and browsing for suppliers is often an enjoyable way to flout your employer's internet policy.

However, when you're getting married in a different way, your method of planning needs to be different too. You can still plan the wedding yourself of course, but you'll find the experience of shopping for suppliers in a different country (and in a different language) infinitely more challenging. You can't pop to the new hairdresser in town and have a few trial up-dos, for example, and I can tell you from experience that Italian patisseries rarely have websites showing examples of their wedding cakes. And although it's not the most important aspect of your day, you probably don't want to realise on the morning of your wedding that you've failed to explain to your Italian-speaking florist what "teardrop" means.

Of course, all these are all moot points if you know your area particularly well and are fluent in the language, but otherwise you're probably going to need a little help. All in all there are three different planning methods available to you: tour operators, wedding co-ordinators or "do it yourself" The different options fulfil different requirements, and when choosing you should think carefully about what kind of wedding you want and how much time you're prepared to put into planning. If you're still undecided, try the following quick quiz: it might give you a few ideas:

1. Are you looking forward to planning your wedding?	
I'd like the wedding planning to be relaxed and I don't necessarily want to get involved in all the details - I'd rather arrive and find it all arranged	A
I'm looking forward to planning the wedding for the most part, but some aspects sound a bit daunting	B
Totally. I can't wait to throw myself in and get completely immersed	C

2. How would you like to liaise with your suppliers?	
I'm happy to tell someone else what I want and let them make the bookings and sort out the details on my behalf	A
I'd like to have some choice and perhaps shop around, but I'm not confident enough to call suppliers and negotiate prices	B
I'd like to liaise with the suppliers directly and keep tabs on all aspects at all times	C

3. What is your wedding budget like?	
One of the reasons I'm getting married abroad is to keep the budget as low as possible	A
I expect to pay less than I would do for an equivalent wedding at home, but it isn't a priority to keep the budget as low as possible	B
The budget is not an issue	C

4. How personalised do you want your wedding to be?	
I have a colour scheme in mind and know generally what I want	A
I know exactly what theme or style I want, down to the type of flowers, music, menus etc.	B
My wedding will be highly personalised – I know exactly what I want, right down to specific suppliers	C

5. How would you like your wedding to be planned overall?	
I'm confident in leaving the arrangements to a company that is well placed to make bookings on my behalf	A
I'd like to be a little more hands-on, although I'd like to have one point of contact who knows me and what my requirements are, all the way through the planning process and on the day	B
I'd like to be the sole point of contact – I don't want to rely on anyone else	C

6. How long are you intending to stay in the resort before or after the wedding?	
We'll book holiday for a week or two and have the wedding and honeymoon in the resort	A
I don't intend to spend more than a week in the resort	B
I am able to arrive at the resort at least four days before the wedding day, and will be available there for a couple of days afterwards	C

7. What's your idea of the perfect holiday?	
I like package holidays, with everything planned and in place before I go.	A
I like to book flights and hotels separately, finding those ideal hotels not necessarily in the holiday brochures	B
I'm not afraid to go off the beaten track, and am comfortable chatting with locals to find the best places to stay	C

Mostly As:
Tour Operators
Average Wedding Package Price: £700 approx

Overview
When European marriage laws changed, tour operators were quick to spot the opportunity to offer added value to their holiday packages, and with the travel and hotel services already in place, they quickly established dedicated teams to deal with the nuptial aspects. It's easy to see how these companies could smoothly extend their package holidays into weddings abroad, and they certainly have a great deal of experience in arranging travel and offer some very competitive prices. Always bear in mind that tour operators are just that – tour operators first and foremost, so if you are getting married abroad to escape the hassle of a wedding at home and just want to turn up to a pre-organised, pre-defined day as part of a holiday in the sun, then this style of wedding will be perfect for you.

The Co-ordination
Almost all tour operators cater for weddings now, and they do so in different ways, from catch-all "package weddings" to personalised services more akin to a private co-ordinator. Some have a large team of people based in the UK who will deal with your query and help with your planning in the run-up to the wedding, whilst some offer you one dedicated point of contact. These co-ordinators are highly experienced as they deal with many weddings each year, although they may not specialise in a particular area, or have the scope to offer different styles.

As soon as you get to your destination, you and your booking will be transferred to the company's local co-ordinator who will usually be working alone. This could either be a dedicated employee of your tour operator, or a local independent wedding co-ordinator hired by your tour operator for that purpose. Once there, the local co-ordinator will confirm the date and time of your wedding (if this hasn't already been done) and arrange your flowers, hairdresser, wedding cake, and any other extras you may have booked. These bookings will be made with the company's preferred suppliers.

Questions to ask:
- Will I have one dedicated point of contact throughout the planning process?
- Will that person also be my contact in the resort?
- If not, who will that person be?

Time Scales
Most tour operators require you to book at least 12 weeks prior to your requested wedding date, and some will only arrange weddings between the months of May and September.

Tour operators and co-ordinators present all their requested dates to the local Town Hall who endeavour to facilitate as many people's choices as possible. Some tour operators are very good at confirming your date and time as soon as they know them; however, some companies will not do so until you arrive at the resort. If your chosen company does have restrictions such as these they probably won't present a problem for you if you're travelling alone or with a small party, but if some of your guests will be flying out just for the wedding day it could be impossible for them to book in advance. In some cases you may even find you have to spend two weeks in the resort, with your wedding taking place on the day before you leave.

Some tour operators will also require you to fulfil certain residency requirements, often accepting the booking only as part of a package holiday of pre-determined length. Despite this, do bear in mind that Italy has no legal residency requirements, and these timescales are solely a condition of the individual companies, or of the hotel at which you are staying.

Questions to ask:
- Can you guarantee my requested wedding date and time?
- **When will I find out what my confirmed wedding date and time is?**
- What are the residency requirements, and how many days will I have to stay in resort?
- Do you offer group discounts for wedding guests?
- Does my chosen hotel have a minimum stay requirement?

The Style
Because the tour operator will use preferred suppliers, your scope to personalise your wedding will exist within these limitations. There are similarities to their holiday packages in that they offer a range of hotels, flights and suppliers, and you'll be able to choose within this range. The basics will follow a set formula, however, and your wedding could well be one of many held on the same day in the same location. In peak season, the most popular civil wedding venues in Italy can conduct up to 10 weddings in a day, so you may find yourself part of a wedding "conveyor-belt", with newlyweds coming out of your venue as you wait to go in.

> *Questions to ask:*
> - Will I have a choice of suppliers, and will I have the opportunity to see examples of their work?
> - When will the suppliers be booked?
> - How many weddings are likely to be taking place at our venue on our wedding day, and will they be held adjacent to ours?
> - Are there any other wedding receptions taking place at our reception venue?

The Cost
As well as being the easiest to arrange, this option is usually the cheapest in terms of the wedding package price, but don't forget that on top of the wedding cost you'll probably need to budget for a package holiday for a duration specified by the company. Tour operators use block bookings to secure best prices, so if cost and effort are all things you want to keep to a minimum, and you want to combine the wedding with a package holiday, this is the choice for you.

> *Questions to ask:*
> - What items are included in the package price?
> - What items can be arranged at extra cost, and what are the approximate prices?
> - If a package holiday needs to be booked in conjunction with the wedding, what are the approximate prices?
> - Can you make hotel bookings and arrange transfers for the wedding party and guests?
> - Do you offer group discounts for these services?
> - Can you help with sightseeing and tourist information for the guests?

Tour Operator Matrix

For Weddings in Italy	Approx cost	Consular & registry fees. Legal paperwork. Translator	On-site co-ordinator	Wedding day Transportation	Posy for Bride & Buttonhole for Groom	Wedding cake
Citalia	From £899	✓	✓	£	✓	✓
Cosmos	From £589	✓	✓	£	✓	✓
Cresta	From £899	✓	✓	£	✓	£
First Choice	From £479	✓	✓	£	✓	✓
Kirker	From £1200	✓	✓	✓	£	£
Kuoni	From £798	✓	✓	✓	✓	✓
Magic of Italy	From £655	✓	✓	£	✓	£
Thomas Cook	From £699	✓	✓	£	£	£
Thomson	From £385	✓	✓	£	✓	✓

✓ Included in package price
x Service not available
£ Service available at extra cost

Photo, Video, Hairdressing & Beautician	Religious Ceremonies Available	Civil Ceremonies Available	Min booking period	Time and date confirmed	Minimum stay requirements
£	✓	✓	12 weeks	Around 6 months prior to wedding date	
£	x	✓	12 weeks	Around 6 months prior to wedding date	Arrive 4 days before. Must be part of 2 week package holiday
£	✓	✓	12 weeks	At time of booking	2-3 working days before wedding. Otherwise no min stay, apart from that which some hotels stipulate
£	x	✓	12 weeks	Near to date of departure. Date & time subject to late changes	Must be part of package holiday. Wedding takes place during 2nd week of holiday.
£	x	✓	12 weeks		Part of 7 night package holiday
£	x	✓	12 weeks	Usually within 7 days of booking	Five working days prior to wedding. Part of 8 night holiday package
£	✓	✓	12 weeks	Either in Jan, or a couple of weeks after booking	4 working days before. Must be part of package holiday
£	x	✓	12 weeks	Date confirmed prior to travel	0 to 4 working days prior to wedding. Part of 14 night package.
£	x	✓	12 weeks	Venue, time and date may not be confirmed until arrival. May also be subject to late changes	Part of 14 night package holiday

*Please note that this information was taken from the relevant tour operator brochures at time of print and is intended as a general guide only. We strongly advise you check all details with each tour operator before making your decision.

Mostly Bs:
Wedding Co-ordinators
Average Wedding Package Price: £800 approx

Overview
A happy medium between tour operators and DIY planning, wedding co-ordinators offer a range of packages which allow you to either plan the wedding yourself, giving you as much or as little help as you need, or can take over and plan the entire event whilst creating a bespoke wedding to suit you. Generally a little more expensive than tour operators, the price you pay will differ greatly depending on whether you use them to plan and co-ordinate your entire wedding, or just use them for certain aspects (even using them just to handle the legal paperwork if you prefer the DIY approach). They allow you to be as hands-on as you want to be, and your wedding is guaranteed to be unique to you, allowing you to book out of season and use some of the lesser-known hotels and venues.

The Co-ordination
There are three kinds of company that you'll come across: planning companies that have offices in the UK, US or Ireland and manage the arrangements from there, companies based in Italy that provide a country-wide service, or local companies based in your chosen location and specialising in that particular region.

Most wedding planning companies have very small teams (sometimes even working alone) and you'll normally deal with the same person throughout the process. That person will plan with you in the run up to the wedding and will often continue that support on a one-to-one basis when you arrive at the venue, also acting as your on-the-day co-ordinator. In this way you are guaranteed familiarity and continuity. Co-ordinators are likely to be extremely au fait with the legalities and paperwork needed, and will be able to liaise with your suppliers in person, on your behalf, rather than you having to struggle over the phone in a different language. They can also act as an interpreter for the different customs and traditions that you may not be aware of.

> *Questions to ask:*
> - Where is the company based?
> - How long has the company been operating and what is its experience?
> - Will I have one dedicated point of contact throughout the planning process?
> - Does the service include on-the-day co-ordination?
> - Am I able to obtain references from recent customers?

Time Scales

Planners are very flexible – many can arrange weddings at very short notice as they can present all your paperwork to the Town Hall as quickly as you can courier it to them. They work all year round, so you'll be able to book out of the busy peak season.

Planners will present your requested dates to the Town Hall and will usually let you know as soon as they receive confirmation, which leaves you (or them) free to arrange your invitations and book your other suppliers. Remember that if you book a co-ordinator based in the same area as your wedding venue, they may well receive a priority service from the Town Hall who will often know them personally.

There should be no residency requirements when you book with a planner, who will present your documents to the Town Hall on your behalf, leaving you free to arrive in Italy as close to your wedding date as you like.

Questions to ask:
- Can you guarantee my requested wedding date and time?
- When will I find out what my confirmed wedding date and time is?
- Do you have any residency requirements?
- How long do you need to arrange my wedding?

©JoAnne Dunn Photographer

The Style

This is entirely of your making! If you hand the entire arrangements over to your planner, they will establish your preferred style and continually check with you to ensure they are on track. On the other hand you can work alongside your planner using their recommendations and contacts to tailor the perfect wedding for you at your planner's preferred rates, or you can use your planner just for your legal and translation requirements and source your own suppliers. A whole range is open to you and you'll have a good choice of locations and suppliers at your disposal, often known personally to your planner.

Planners are also able to make hotel bookings on your behalf, and arrange guest services and sightseeing.

Questions to ask:
- Who are your preferred suppliers, and will I have the opportunity to see examples of their work?
- When will the suppliers be booked?
- Are you able to liaise with any suppliers that I source myself, i.e. other than those on your preferred list?
- Can you make hotel bookings and arrange transfers for the guests?
- Do you offer group discounts for these services?
- Can you help with sightseeing and tourist information for the guests?

The Cost

The pricing structures of co-ordinators vary. Some charge flat fees for their basic services, adding costs for each additional service you require, some offer a range of tiered packages you can choose from, others charge a percentage of your overall wedding budget. Generally however, the prices do not compare with those of UK wedding planners, who tend to be far more expensive.

Questions to ask:
- Does the company charge a flat rate, or a percentage of the total wedding spend?
- Does the company offer a tiered package service, or an ad hoc service?

Mostly Cs:
DIY Planning

Overview
If you decide to plan your wedding with no outside help, you'll be sure to retain overall control, but if you're going for this option you need to be experienced in event co-ordination, enjoy juggling tasks and not be afraid of a challenge! Clearly a pretty tall order, but this is sure to be a rewarding project. The legal process is relatively straightforward (although the bureaucracy can be time consuming) and there are plenty of suppliers available around the country, many of which are listed in this series.

The Co-ordination
You'll be the sole point of contact for all your suppliers and you'll be responsible for sorting out any problems and negotiating prices and contracts. You will also need to be prepared to make trips to various embassies to sort out the legal paperwork in an environment notorious for its red tape and bureaucracy. Inevitably you'll also need to make at least one, if not several, trips to your destination during the planning process, unless you have family or friends in the area who can act on your behalf.

Time Scales
Start planning as early as possible and leave plenty of time to get all your paperwork in place. Allow yourself and your witnesses around four days in the country before the wedding date in order to present your documents at the Town Hall and receive your *Nulla Osta*. You ought also to ensure you have at least a week in the location after your wedding to enable you to chase up your wedding certificate. However, these tasks can be done on your behalf if you have friends or family in the area willing to help. Likewise, you can hire a co-ordinator to handle these aspects alone.

The Style
Again, you have full reign on style. Make sure you are as familiar with local customs and traditions as possible, as they are likely to be very different to those at home and your expectations may not otherwise be fulfilled.

The Cost
You may assume that this will be the cheapest option, but this is not always the case. You're unlikely to be able to negotiate the kind of supplier discounts that co-ordinators or tour operators can, and you must remember to take account of the costs involved in the frequent overseas phone calls and trips to the location.
If you do decide on planning your wedding in this way, it is as well to have the number of a co-ordinator close by in case you need a helping hand with any of the aspects.

Types of Ceremony

"Somehow you don't realise you're not saying any vows during the civil ceremony. The articles of law are so perfect I can't imagine anyone not being happy with them."
Amalfi Coast Bride

It's important to know that only two types of ceremony are legally binding in Italy: Civil Ceremonies and Catholic Ceremonies. You can hold a non-Catholic religious ceremony (or blessing), although as it will not be legally binding you also will need to hold a Civil Ceremony beforehand either in Italy or at home.

The Civil Ceremony

Civil Ceremonies in Italy must be conducted in premises owned by the local Town Hall and, in most cases, this will be the Town Hall itself. I know this conjures up images of dull, bureaucratic, thread-bare rooms, but fear not! Italian Town Halls are vastly different from the ones you find in the UK, and are usually very elegant and ornate.

In some towns you may find that the Town Hall owns an additional property - in Sorrento, for example, the Town Hall also owns the 13th Century St Francesco Monastery Cloisters. Be wary of companies offering hotels and private houses for the ceremony - if you want to go for one of these options, check with the Town Hall that your marriage will be legally binding.

The ceremony will last between 15 and 25 minutes, and you are usually allowed to personalise it with a short reading and your own music. It is a legal obligation for all non-Italian residents to have the ceremony translated by an official interpreter even if you both speak Italian - this is normally a service that your co-ordinator will provide.

The format is, of course, different to that of a UK Civil Ceremony so it's important not to make any assumptions about the service based on the ceremonies you're used to. There is no "you may now kiss the bride", for example, and the exchanging of the rings is a very important, legally binding part of the ceremony (so if you weren't planning on having wedding rings, make sure you borrow some for the day!).

Civil Ceremony Format

The ceremony will be conducted by a local civil official with an official interpreter to translate the ceremony into English. Once everyone has arrived (essentially the couple plus two witnesses), the ceremony will begin.

Instead of making vows, the official will read out three articles of Italian law relating to marriage. These will each be translated in turn, and are as follows:

Celebrant: "Are you <groom's name>?"
Groom: "I am"
Celebrant: "And are you <bride's name>?"
Bride: "I am"

Celebrant:
"In accordance with the law of this office, I will now read the civil law that regulates the duties and rights concerning both spouses.

Art. 143
With marriage, husband and wife acquire the same rights and assume the same duties.

The reciprocal obligation of faithfulness, moral and material assistance, collaboration in the interest of the family and cohabitation, all derive from the rite of matrimony.

Both spouses have a duty, each in relationship to their patrimony, professional or domestic capacities, to contribute to the needs of the family.

Art. 144
The spouses must agree on the management of the family and fix the family residence according to both their needs and those pre-eminent to the family itself. Each consort has the right to decide on the management of the family as agreed.

Art. 147
The rite of matrimony obliges both spouses to maintain, instruct and educate their offspring to their natural inclinations and aspirations."

Celebrant: "Do you <groom's name> take the here present <bride's name> to be your lawful wife?"
Groom: "I do"

Celebrant: "And do you <bride's name> take the here present <groom's name> to be your lawful husband?"
Bride: "I do"

Celebrant: "Have both witnesses heard?"
Witnesses: "We have"

Celebrant: "In the name of the law I now pronounce <groom's name> and <bride's name> husband and wife."

Bride and Groom exchange rings

Bride, Groom and Witnesses sign the relevant paperwork, and the celebrant will summarise the ceremony.

After the ceremony, the guests usually exit first while you have the option of having a few photos taken in the venue. The guests congregate outside ready with the confetti, waiting for you to make your big exit.

If you want to insert a reading, you may do so at any point. I'd suggest having one between the end of the ceremony and the exchanging of the rings, or between the exchanging of the rings and the signing of the paperwork. The reading must contain no religious content and be fairly short in length - civil ceremonies have to work within rigid time slots, especially if another couple is waiting to get married after you.

So as you can see it's pretty short and if you're considering having music during the ceremony you'll need to think carefully about the length of your pieces and where to have them. Many couples select a few pieces of music and have them playing throughout the ceremony; this works well as there aren't really any gaps during the ceremony and, if you're holding your ceremony in a public venue, it helps to drown out the shuffling of any unexpected guests.

Incidentally, don't ask me what the missing **Art. 145** and **Art. 146** contain. I've tried to convince my husband that they have something to do with him making me tea on demand, but it hasn't worked.

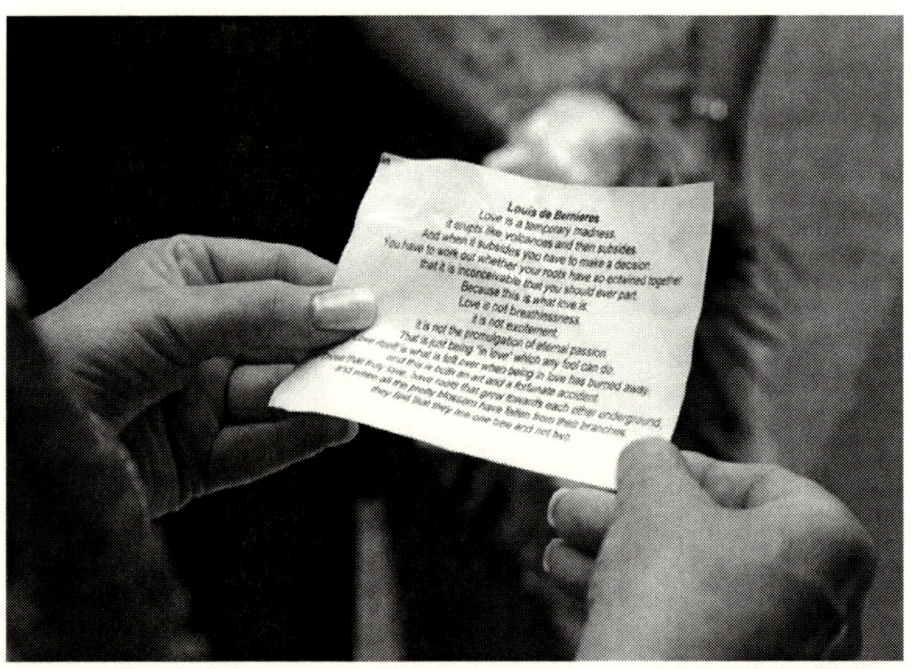

© JoAnne Dunn Photographer

Religious Ceremonies

The Catholic wedding ceremony is the only religious ceremony that is recognised as legally binding, as it is the only religious ceremony that fulfils both the civil and legal requirements. For all other religious ceremonies, you will need to hold a civil wedding first.

Catholic Ceremonies

Catholic ceremonies may only be performed inside a Catholic church. Depending on where you get married they can be fairly difficult to arrange, as it's becoming increasingly common for priests in Italy to refuse to marry non-Italians. If you have your heart set on a Catholic ceremony, the first thing you will need to do is speak to your parish priest, as he will need to seek permission from the Archbishop from whom you must gain Special Dispensation to marry outside of your parish. At the same time, get in touch with a co-ordinator to establish whether there are any priests in your desired area who are prepared to marry non-Italians, and who can perform the ceremony in English.

Once this step has been completed, you will need to fulfil all the *Pre Cana* requirements usual for a UK wedding. Your priest will need to provide written confirmation that these have been completed, as well as his permission for you to marry outside of the parish along with the Special Dispensation from the Archbishop. These then need to be sent to the Italian church with your birth, baptismal, communion and confirmation certificates.

If only one of you is Catholic, you will again need to gain special dispensation from your Archbishop to enter into a mixed marriage. If either of you have been divorced, you must first obtain an annulment before you may marry again in a Catholic Church. This is an involved procedure that typically takes around two years to complete.

You need to be aware that a full set of paperwork and dispensations does not guarantee you a Catholic wedding, as the final decision rests with the priest of your chosen church in Italy. If you find yourself coming up against problems, remember that you can always opt to hold a civil wedding first and then hold a Catholic blessing (a Convalidation), which is almost identical in appearance to a Catholic wedding ceremony except that there is no signing of the register.

If you're a Catholic, then the ceremony and the Mass will be very familiar to you and probably won't need explaining; after all, it's the same world-wide. However if you're marrying a Catholic or you just need a reminder, then here is a brief synopsis of the wedding service:

Introductory Rites - Opening prayers and a welcome to the couple and guests
Readings - Biblical readings perhaps by one of the guests
Gospel – Biblical reading by the priest
Homily - A sermon given by the priest, usually about the nature of marriage

Rite of Marriage - The vows. There will be a few to choose from, which you should have decided on with the priest beforehand
Exchanging of Rings - After all the "I do"s, the rings will be blessed and exchanged.
Nuptial Mass - The Sign of Peace takes place and the rite of Holy Communion follows. The priest closes the ceremony with a prayer and nuptial blessing. He presents the couple as husband and wife before announcing the end of the Mass.

More information on Catholic Weddings can be found at
www.marriagecare.org.uk

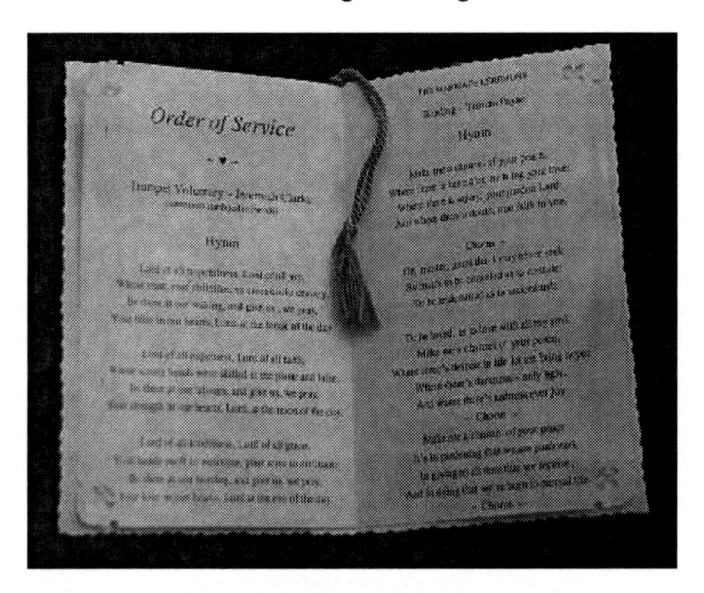

Protestant, Jewish & Other Religious Ceremonies
As the Catholic ceremony is the only legally recognised religious wedding ceremony in Italy, all other ceremonies would be considered symbolic only and therefore a civil ceremony must have taken place first either at home or in Italy. The religious ceremony can be held in any location (including gardens and hotels), but if you wish to hold the ceremony in a religious building it is advisable to arrange the wedding through a co-ordinator who will be able to contact the relevant religious institutions and establish the individual paperwork requirements.

You must fulfil any pre-marital requirements specified by your parish church or place of worship and, if relevant and permitted, receive dispensation to marry if either of you are divorced or if you are of mixed religions.

Information on Church of England Weddings can be found at
www.cofe.anglican.org.

For information on Jewish weddings go to www.judaism.com and
www.jmc-uk.org

Symbolic Ceremonies and Renewal of Vows

A Symbolic or Renewal of Vows ceremony is not legally binding, but is a chance for you to publicly declare your commitment to each other. It can be conducted anywhere you wish by a person of your choosing, and all without the need to fulfil legal requirements - an aspect which makes this type of ceremony popular with those who are prepared to hold a (sometimes secret) civil ceremony at home beforehand (the guests are usually none the wiser!). Any co-ordinator and most hotel venues will be able to make the necessary arrangements and help you plan the order of the day.

Same-sex Partnerships

At the time of writing, same-sex partnership registration is still unavailable in Italy, so you would need to hold the ceremony in the UK first before arranging a Symbolic ceremony in Italy.

More information on Symbolic Ceremonies, Renewal of Vows and Same-sex Partnerships can be found at www.civilceremonies.co.uk

Customs, Traditions and Etiquette

"It's a tradition in some parts of Italy to walk to the venue together, and we liked the idea. And it was lovely, walking hand in hand through Sorrento with our attendants behind as people stopped to watch us pass".

Sorrento Bride

Of course not everyone does weddings the way the Brits do, and with some crucial differences between Italian and English weddings it's important to understand what these are when you're talking to suppliers. For example, did you know that in Italy the top table consists only of the bride and groom, and the word "confetti" in Italian refers to sugared almonds? And yes, they do throw them at you when you're coming out of the venue (it's ok – they know not to aim at your heads).

So at the risk of sounding like an HSBC ad, and bearing in mind that traditions and superstitions can vary between regions, here are some common ones you can use to add a real Italian flavour to your day:

Italian "Confetti"

Italian Traditions
Meeting
Some Italians you speak to will strongly deny the existence of this custom, but the truth is that years ago in some parts of Italy (mainly in the Veneto) the bride and groom would walk to the venue, either together or individually. It's not a tradition that has been particularly well preserved, and the thought of sullying fine clothes by traipsing through the streets would give most modern Italians hot flushes. However, it is still an old custom and a very romantic one at that; your "first sight" moment will be private and more intimate, and you'll have the opportunity to spend a few quiet minutes together before the whirlwind of the day begins. And if you're inspired more by practicalities than by romance, consider the money you'll save on a wedding car.

In days gone by the walk to the church was an important part of the day and it incorporated a number of tests and superstitions along the way.
The custom seems to have two variations. In one, the groom or his mother buys the bride a bouquet before proceeding with the family to the bride's home. The future in-laws greet each other, the groom presents his future wife with her bouquet, and the group walks to the ceremony together.

The other (much more conservative) variation is where the bride and her family arrive at the venue where they are met by the groom and his mother who are waiting outside with the bouquet. In some regions brides can even expect to see all the guests congregated outside awaiting her arrival, although in most parts of Italy now the "UK" format is followed, with the groom waiting inside and the bride being "given away" by her father.

Another tradition is for the mother of the groom to enter the church with her son who ushers her to her seat, an important event that will generally spark off a round of photographs. Another nice tradition involves the bride plucking a bloom from her bouquet and presenting it to the groom's mother just before the start of the ceremony.

The groom making a gift of his bride's bouquet has proved to be an enduring tradition, although these days it's usually delivered by the florist on the morning of the wedding.

Italian Superstitions

To Bring Luck

Italian weddings are packed with superstition from start to finish, seemingly even more so than in the UK. If you are of a superstitious nature then you may find yourself facing a bit of a dilemma; do the English rules apply to you because you're English, or do you have to incorporate the ones that apply to weddings on Italian turf? Do you, heaven forbid, have to include both? My advice would be to cherry-pick the ones that mean something to you or the ones that look the most fun, and go with it. You probably know most of the English ones, so here is a list of a few Italian superstitions said to bring you luck:

- For the very best luck, hold your wedding on a Sunday in June.
- It's considered lucky for the bride to wear green on the night before the wedding.
- Don't be too upset if you wake up on your wedding day to see rain - the Italians have an old saying: "*sposa bagnata, sposa fortunata*" – literally "A wet bride is a lucky bride"!
- When the bride leaves her residence she should cut a white ribbon tied across the gate or doorway.
- The groom should carry a piece of iron in his pocket to ward off bad luck.
- Don't worry if some of your guests wear black – it's no problem in Italy. The big no-no instead is lilac.
- It's unlucky for the bride to wear gold before or during the ceremony.
- One of the most potent symbols of good luck in Italy is the *corno* – a little red horn believed to ward off bad luck.

Italian "*Corni*"

Major Differences

Superstitions are not the only things that vary between countries; traditional events during the day differ too. Of course you can export a full UK wedding if that is your preference, but you might find it fun to include some of these Italian differences:

- Italians throw rice and sugared almonds instead of paper or petal confetti (although this is starting to become popular).
- Welcome drinks are typically prosecco or bellini (especially in Venice). On the Amalfi Coast, Limoncello is offered as an after-dinner drink. Bear in mind that excessive drinking is frowned upon in Italy – drunkenness at receptions certainly isn't the norm, and if you are holding your reception in a public place then expect a certain amount of disapproval if any of your guests are clearly over the limit.
- Italian weddings don't really have receiving lines as the bride and groom tend to arrive at the reception after their guests, having had some photographs taken alone just after the ceremony.
- Italians don't have the same heavy fruit based wedding cake that we have. Wedding cakes tend to be made of cream (more like a gateaux), and although the regional specialties vary, you can choose whichever type you like, from Rum Baba, to profiterole towers, to chocolate, strawberry or lemon cream cakes. If the supplier is informed that the cake is for a wedding you can expect it to be beautifully decorated.

Delizie al Limone - a typical wedding cake in the South of Italy

- Traditional favours consist of sugared almonds (always given in odd numbers) usually presented in small ceramic pots which are taken away as keepsakes.
- A typical reception starts with pre-dinner drinks and canapés followed by the meal. Traditional Italian receptions consist of many, many courses, but if you are booking a standard reception at a hotel or restaurant you can expect to be served five courses – antipasti, pasta or risotto, meat, fish, and dessert or pudding (usually the wedding cake).
- The bride and groom sit together on the top table, mingling among the tables between courses.
- During the reception, the groom's tie is cut into tiny pieces and auctioned to the guests. The money raised is given to the bride and groom.
- Whenever the guests clap and cheer, it is a signal for the newlyweds to kiss.
- Upon leaving the reception, the bride and groom should stamp on a glass – the number of pieces is said to represent the number of years the marriage will last.
- It is usual to provide food for the photographers. Also, it's highly unusual for guests to pay for their own drinks.
- Often there isn't dancing and only background music is provided, although some weddings will feature bands. DJs are very rare. If you're looking for an alternative, most UK couples (especially those with fewer guests) compile a CD which can be used as both background and dancing music. These tend to be themed and typically have an Italian flavour, with music such as Il Divo, Rat Pack, swing or jazz.

Invitations

Some couples who decide to get married abroad do so because of potential tensions at home, and it's these couples in particular that tend to worry about their guest list. In reality, it's usually only your nearest and dearest who'll take the time, spend the money and make the effort to attend your wedding, and it's highly unlikely that more distant relatives and casual friends (or people just looking for a free meal and a bit of trouble) are going to bother; in fact, on average, you can expect around a 30% to 40% acceptance rate. For this reason, it's a good idea to send your invitations out in waves; that way you'll be able to keep control of the numbers a little better, sending out subsequent waves if it looks like your guests are going to be thin on the ground. Don't forget to send invitations to those who you know will be unable to come, as some people (especially elderly relatives) will take offence if they do not receive a formal invitation.

As your guests will have to make special arrangements to attend your wedding abroad, you're going to need to send your invitations out somewhat earlier than you would if you were holding a wedding at home. You can give your guests an early heads-up by sending save-the-date cards but be aware that, while this might seem like the perfect solution, it may well lead to some confusion for your guests: it's easy to simply "save the date" for an event at home, but until your guests receive and accept a formal invitation for a wedding abroad, they are going to wonder whether it's necessary for them to start booking flights, hotels and time off work. Of course it goes without saying that any guests you do send save-the-dates to should automatically receive an invitation.

My advice, if you are sending save-the-date cards, is to do so around nine months before the wedding date and to make the situation clear. In other words, if you don't know the exact time and date of the wedding because you've booked with a tour operator that doesn't release this information until nearer the time, then indicate this in your correspondence. If the date and time is subject to change, then indicate this also. I'd suggest wording along the following lines:

Please save the date of
31st May 2007
for the wedding of
Henriette & Giacomo
to be held in Venice, Italy

Exact time and date to be confirmed.
Information to follow, or visit our wedding website for further details:
www.amarriagemade.co.uk

With respect to your invitations, these should be sent to all save-the-date recipients as soon as you receive confirmation of your date and time. Alternatively, if you've booked with a co-ordinator, you can send your save-the-dates with a full set of information or skip that step and issue your invitations right away. You'll still need to do this in plenty of time in order to allow people to book their flights, and although you can never give people too much notice I think six months is a reasonable amount of time. Again, wording would follow the UK format, for example:

Mr & Mrs de Schnetzmann
request the pleasure of the company of

_____

at the marriage of their daughter

Henriette
to
Mr Giacomo Casanova

at Palazzo Cavalli, Venezia
on Thursday 31st May, 2007
at 3.00pm

and afterwards at
Ca'Zanardi, Cannaregio, Venezia

1 Wimpole Street   *R.S.V.P*
London   *31st March 2007*
W1 5ST

www.amarriagemade.co.uk

An invitation for a reception back on home turf might look like this:

Mr & Mrs de Schnetzmann
request the pleasure of the company of

_____

at a reception to celebrate the marriage
of their daughter

Henriette
to
Mr Giacomo Casanova

which took place at
Palazzo Cavalli, Venezia
on Thursday 31st May, 2007

Please join us in celebration of the event
on Saturday 9th June, 2007
at 5.00pm
at
The Colonnade Hotel, Little Venice, London

1 Wimpole Street   *R.S.V.P*
London   *31st March 2007*
W1 5ST
www.amarriagemade.co.uk

Information Websites

With a traditional UK wedding it is usual to enclose an information sheet with the invitations, giving basic advice on things like directions, parking, accommodation and the like. Try to do this with a wedding abroad, and your carefully designed invitation is likely to get lost in a stack of paperwork.

The ideal solution is to set up a wedding information website which can be constantly added to and updated, keeping your guests in the loop and even providing them with a format through which they can contact you and other guests. Those guests without internet access can always receive a hard-copy of the information in the time-honoured tradition. After the wedding, and if you've bought your own domain name, the website is a useful place to post messages of thanks, wedding reports and of course all the photos.

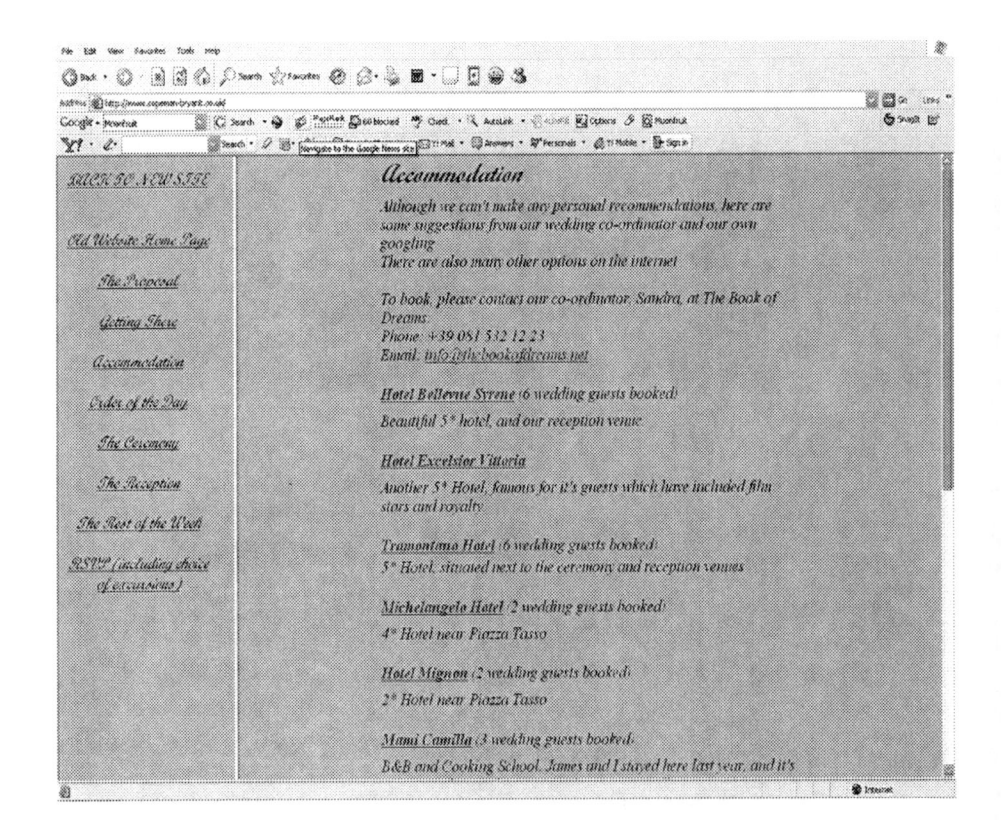

When designing your site, put yourself in your guests' shoes. Try to imagine you've never been to the destination before, you're travelling under your own steam and don't know what to expect when you get there. The kind of information you really need to add includes such things as:

- Flight information
- How to get from the airport to the resort (including bus and train timetables and taxi information)
- Recommended accommodation
- Timings for the wedding day
- Tourist information
- Dress code

If you or someone you know can design websites from scratch then all this won't present much of a challenge. However, if you don't know a thing about HTML, DreamWeaver or FrontPage, fear not – there are dozens of websites that can do it all for you with a few clicks of a mouse, and are very reasonably priced or even free if you don't mind your site being splattered with ads. Take a look at the following services which provide a variety of styles, methods and prices.

www.thehitchingpost.co.uk
www.weddingpath.co.uk
www.moonfruit.co.uk
www.weddingwindow.com
www.myevent.com
www.ewedding.com
www.wedquarters.com
http://easily.co.uk/wedding_websites.html

Gifts

It's a tricky decision: as your wedding guests will have to pay a fair amount to attend your wedding, should you expect them to put the time, effort and money into attending and then ask them to give you a gift on top? It might be considered a little cheeky, but on the other hand there will be many more people who won't be able to attend and who will want to buy you something as a token. What do you do?

This is a contentious subject at the best of times, but even more so when your wedding is overseas. Etiquette concerning the matter of gifts is rapidly developing, and only you know what will or won't offend your guests - the only advice is to think carefully and use your best judgement. One of the best ideas seems to be to have an unpublicised "contingency" gift list, only to be given to those not attending the wedding (or those insisting on attending *and* buying) if and when they ask for it. Many couples do this, and confirm that parental word-of-mouth is very effective in ensuring the information gets to the right people, while at the same time it avoids putting the onus on the guests to make the decision.

Asking for money is becoming more and more popular, but again think carefully in this situation. It may be that some of your friends or family would like to attend the wedding but can't afford the costs, or it might be that they've had to save hard to be with you on the day. If this is the case they may find it grates a little if you ask them to hand you hard cash as well. Similarly, if someone has paid out for an unscheduled holiday in order to celebrate your day with you, it might seem a little cheeky to ask them to contribute to your honeymoon so that you can afford to go off on another, more exotic holiday.

I would stress that none of these options are "wrong"; it's just that they may be wrong for some people. Use your best judgement and knowledge of the people involved before you make the decision.

Apparel

"Think about how comfortable you will be in your dress and the climate of the host country. You want to wear it effortlessly and easily, for it to feel perfect in every way."
www.weddings-abroad-guide.com

During my research for the Amalfi Coast Area Guide in 2006, I interviewed the manager of a well-known Ravello hotel. While flicking through his album of past-wedding photographs, he stopped at one, a picture of a bride in a strapless, lace-up satin dress and tiara, and a groom in a lightweight, light-coloured suit. "These people are English, as you can see", he said, pointing at the clothes.

If you spend any time in Sorrento, a town full of multi-national weddings, you can spot the nationality of the couple a mile off. None of the Italian guests wear hats or are shy of wearing black for one thing, but what really stands out are the bride and groom. Of course the style of your wedding is up to you, but in case you want to blend in and avoid the "Brits Abroad" syndrome, have a scout around the websites of some Italian photographers, and take a look at what the Italians wear. Bridal fashions, as a rule, tend to be slinky, slim and lightweight with interesting straps, sleeves and necklines (strapless is rather rare, as are tiaras). Grooms are always in smart, dark, morning suits. If you're worried about the heat remember that, in Italy, a spring or autumn wedding will see the same kind of average temperatures that you'd experience at a July or August wedding in the UK. In July or August in Italy, the maximum average would be around 30°C.

Transportation & Logistics

This is one part of the logistical planning that always seems to give brides nightmares, and is one of the most frequently asked questions to pop up in my inbox. My advice is to use a courier like DHL to ship items like table decorations, favours and, if it's impossible to carry it with you personally, your wedding dress. If you are taking the dress with you on the flight, my advice is to avoid putting it in the hold, not because something terrible might happen to it (it probably won't), but because you'll never achieve true peace of mind otherwise (and with sod's law being what it is, if one piece of luggage is destined to go missing it'll doubtless be the dress). Men's suits are less of an issue because it's far easier to pick up a decent, off-the-peg replacement at the destination. The chances are it'll be of a better cut and quality anyway.

Airlines, however, are reluctant to let you carry your dress on board with the due deference you would wish. Low-cost airlines certainly won't accommodate hung dresses, and you'll even have trouble if you're travelling First Class on a charter flight as many cabins don't have the facility to hang such a large item. A suit carrier would be ideal if only you could find one big enough to hold a wedding dress and with the ability to fold up into the airlines required dimensions. I'm afraid that the only other option is to squash your dress into a small, carry-on suitcase (no more than 55x40x20cm) that can fit into an overhead locker. It's an uncomfortable prospect, I know, but it's probably not unlike the way it was transported from the manufacturer to the retailer in the first place, and the dress will really be none the worse for it. Make sure the suitcase is clean, and use tissue paper to protect the fabric and minimise creasing. Lay the dress face down with the centre of the dress in the case, making sure it is as flat as possible, then gradually fold in the train and bodice, adding tissue between each fold of fabric. If you can't fit your hoops or underskirts in, and in the event the case you pack them in goes missing, get in touch with the local wedding dress shops when you arrive; it's quite likely that they'll be able to source you something suitable.

Any hotel worth its salt will be able to arrange for the dress and veil to be professionally steamed or pressed on arrival or, failing that, you can easily steam them yourself in your bathroom. To do this, hang the dress or veil as high as possible, close the windows and doors, and run all the hot taps to make the room as steamy as possible. Leave the dress in this environment for a good ten minutes, after which time the creases should have gently dropped out.

©JoAnne Dunn Photographer

When storing your dress for long periods of time it needs to be kept in a way that allows the fabric to breathe. A plain, white cotton duvet cover is a perfect storage cover, or take a look at the dress carrier on www.1stcallforweddings.co.uk/shop.html (although this item is fairly transparent so you'll probably want to employ that duvet cover anyway, just to make sure the dress is shielded from prying eyes).

Keeping Cool

If your wedding is in spring or autumn, the temperatures in Italy shouldn't feel too much hotter than those you're used to, but if you've gone for a summer wedding things could get pretty scorching, especially in that big white dress or dark suit! You need to think carefully not only about the fabrics you are wearing, but also about shoes, make-up and even your hair (fresh flowers will wilt in the heat, so consider some silk ones - there are some fabulous ones available on Ebay).

Natural, loose fitting fabrics will keep you cooler of course, but if you simply can't resist that satin, beaded number then you might need to employ a few tricks to keep dry, cool and comfortable. After you've showered on the day of your wedding, cover your body with a regular, non-scented spray deodorant to keep yourself dry all over and prevent any sweat rash. Copious amounts of talcum powder won't go amiss either, and keep a can of Magicool handy (www.magicool.co.uk). If you're susceptible to chafing or sweat rash there is a fantastic product available called Neat Feat 3B Cream, which can be an absolute god-send. Normally only available from Australia or New Zealand, you can get hold of some from the manufacturers at www.neatfeat.co.nz

With regard to shoes, remember that your feet are likely to swell from heat and overuse, so you might want to think twice about tight, closed-in shoes (and while you're at it, when you're choosing your heel-height remember that Italy has an abundance of cobbles!). Rainbow Club is one bridal shoe manufacturer that has a nice collection of comfortable bridal sandals and open shoes.

Make-up is another thing that tends to suffer in the heat: to prevent your carefully tended face from sliding off in a sweaty mess, use a good matte base before you apply your foundation. Ultra Matte Foundation Base from Anthony Braden Cosmetics does an excellent job, and unless you have very dry skin, a liquid to powder finish foundation will help to keep the skin from becoming too shiny, as will a final touch of pressed powder. Waterproof mascara is, of course, essential at all weddings.

Incidentally, if you're in resort for a few days before the wedding, it may be best to wear a strapless top so that any tan lines don't clash with the neck-line of your dress. Bravissimo stock some fantastic ones with inbuilt bras.

Suit Hire

Before weddings abroad became as popular as they are now, it was virtually impossible to find a suit hire company that offered a reasonable extended hire service. Fortunately there's a certain amount of affordable choice now, so if you're on a budget and aren't intending to splash out on a pricey new whistle, these companies are worth a look:

Company	Website	Phone	Prices from	Extended Hire Supplement
Formally Yours	www.formallyyours.co.uk	0116 275 6746	£55	£25 per outfit for up to 2 weeks
Young's	www.youngs-hire.co.uk	020 8327 3005	£45	Standard hire is 4 days. Extra 7 days hire available for £15 per suit.
Debenhams	www.debenhams-formalhire.com	08445 616161	£43	50% of total hire cost for each additional week.
Burton	www.burtonsmenswear.co.uk	0845 121 4514	£35	50% of total cost for each additional week
Moss Bros	www.mossbros.co.uk/hire	020 7447 7200	£45	£10 per outfit per day for up to 7 days. Double standard charge for up to 2 weeks.
Hire Society	www.hire-society.com	0870 780 4316	£59	Basic price is for one week hire. If hire covers two weekends, supplement is one and a half times the basic price for up to 4 weeks.

Information correct as of July 2006

Task List & Planning Tools

"The planning tools in wedding magazines just aren't relevant to weddings abroad. A lot of what needs to be done is still a grey area for me."

Tuscany Bride

We all know that wedding magazines, planning books and bridal internet sites are full of planning checklists, but how many of them are relevant to your wedding? Most lists you'll come across will be tailored to UK weddings and take no account of the intricacies of an overseas event.

So here is a checklist that contains relevant tasks and deadlines. This is based on a twelve-month planning period, but these timescales are a guideline only and most can be adapted to give yourself more (or less) breathing space. I planned my own wedding comfortably over fourteen months, but many people getting married abroad have much tighter deadlines. Having said that, remember that the tourist season in Italy falls between March and November, and that most weddings take place between May and July. If you want to secure the best venues and the best rooms it's advisable to book at least a year in advance.

Twelve Months + to Go

Decide on your location, or come up with a short list of destinations	
Make your announcements	
Decide on your planning method and start researching companies	
Agree on a budget	
Decide whether to have your honeymoon in the same location	
Arrange a preliminary trip to the location if necessary	
If you are having a religious ceremony, make initial contact with your priest or minister	
Book your co-ordinator or tour operator	
Start looking at wedding dresses	
Make sure you both have valid passports	

Eleven Months to Go

Book your accommodation	
Book your ceremony and reception venue	
Establish deadlines for paperwork requirements	
Start to research accommodation for your guests	
Begin searching for a photographer	
Start to research flights	
Consider ordering or making "Save The Date" cards	
Consider setting up a guest information website	
Start researching your honeymoon, if you are having one separately	
Decide on your guest list	

Ten Months to Go

Book your photographer	
Take out wedding insurance	
Book your flights as soon as your wedding date is confirmed to ensure best prices	
Put together your wedding information website if you are having one, including accommodation and logistical information.	
Book your honeymoon, if you are having one separately	
Pay any deposits	

Nine Months to Go

Send out your "Save the Date" Cards	
Start to think about your invitation designs	

Eight Months to Go

Start to think about your evening entertainment	
If you haven't already done so, make an appointment with your Local Registrar to Give Notice according to the Town Hall deadline (or if in the US, make an appointment with your local Italian consular office to make your *atto notorio*)	
Order any documents you may need to Give Notice (birth certificates, etc.), if this has not been done	
Make or order your wedding invitations	

Seven Months to Go

Begin to obtain quotes and make supplier bookings	

Six Months to Go

Start looking at suits for the men. Make reservations if necessary	
Order your wedding dress	
Send your wedding invitations, along with an information pack or information website details	
If in the US, make your *atto notorio* at your local Italian consular office	

Five Months to Go

Research guest excursions	
Make menu choices	
Start to make or order any other wedding stationery	
Start to shop for wedding rings	
Choose your witnesses and obtain copies of their passports	
Copy and collate all legal documentation	

Four Months to Go

Start to plan your hen night	
Make sure you have a confirmed booking for your hairdresser	
Make sure you have a confirmed booking for your florist	
Make sure you have a confirmed booking for your wedding cake	
Make sure you have a confirmed booking for your transportation	
Make sure you have a confirmed booking for your evening entertainment	
Organise your first dress fitting	
Construct your wedding gift list	

Three Months to Go

Give Notice to your local registrar, if you have not already done so.	
Finalise the guest list and send numbers to your co-ordinator or venue	
Make doctor's appointments for honeymoon jabs, if necessary	
Collect Certificate of Authority from local registrar, if you have not already done so	
Copy all legal documentation and courier to co-ordinator or consulate.	
Have your thank you letter templates ready for when your gift list opens	

Ten Weeks to Go

Confirm your menu and final numbers to your venue	
Buy gifts for your attendants	
Make your orders of the day / orders of service	

Nine Weeks to Go

Make your place settings and other paraphernalia, if necessary	

Eight Weeks to Go

Decide on how you will transport your dress and suits to the resort	

Seven Weeks to Go

Arrange your second dress fitting	

Six Weeks to Go

Finalise your table plan	

Five Weeks to Go

Make sure you are familiar with your suppliers terms and conditions, and confirm how and when they want their balances paid	

Four Weeks to Go

Speak to your gift list holder to arrange delivery of gifts	
Make sure all the speeches are written	

Three Weeks to Go

Send your first batch of thank you letters	
Arrange to have your final dress fitting	

Two Weeks to Go

Order any currency you need (don't forget to include the money for balances)	

One Week to Go

Get your hair cut and your nails manicured	
Ship any paraphernalia to your venue	
Send your second batch of thank you letters	
Collect the suits	
Collect your currency	
Make sure all details are finalised with your venue, co-ordinator and suppliers	

In Location

Pay all outstanding balances	
Go for your hair trial	
Confirm timings for the day	
GET MARRIED!	

After the Wedding

Obtain a copy of your marriage certificate from your co-ordinator or Town Hall	
Register your marriage with the GRO on your return to the UK	
Send out your final batch of thank you letters	

Useful Planning Sites

The internet provides some invaluable resources for wedding planning, especially when the wedding is abroad. What follows are some websites offering tools and forums to help you plan your wedding remotely:

Travel and Accommodation Sites:

www.tripadvisor.co.uk	Invaluable for hotel and venue reviews. Sites also have area specific forums so you can ask the local experts all those obscure questions.
www.parkervillas.com/forum/frame.htm	
www.holidaytruths.co.uk	
www.virtualtourist.com	
www.skyscanner.co.uk	Resources for pin-pointing the cheapest flights
www.cheapflights.com	
www.expedia.co.uk	
www.lastminute.com	
www.opodo.co.uk	
www.trenitalia.com	Italian train network
http://mappe.alice.it	Italian road and town maps
www.venere.com	Excellent accommodation site

Bridal Sites:

www.weddings-abroad-guide.com	UK site dedicated to weddings abroad
www.sposi.it	Italian wedding planning site, useful if you can speak a little of the lingo
www.hitched.co.uk	Popular UK bridal sites
www.confetti.co.uk	
www.weddingguide.co.uk	
www.indiebride.com	US site for the less fluffy brides among you
www.weddingsonline.ie	Irish wedding planning site
www.theknot.com	US wedding planning site
www.weddingforum.co.uk	Smaller UK planning sites, but with potentially useful information
www.weddingforums.co.uk	
www.loveweddings.co.uk	

General Information Sites for Italian Weddings

www.italiansrus.com/resources/weddings.htm	Advise on Italian wedding customs
www.virtualitalia.com/articles/wedding.shtml	
www.italy-weddings.com/	
www.italyweddings.com/flowers/season.html	Useful tool for checking what flowers are in season

Other Useful Tools

www.perfecttableplan.com/	Handy table planning software
www.contextures.com/excelfiles.html	

Budget Planner & Finances

"Your money will stretch a lot further abroad than it will at home".

www.weddings-abroad-guide.com

Budget Planner

The cost of a wedding in Italy is significantly less than a wedding in the UK, and you'll certainly get more for your money in terms of quality, originality and wow factor. Included here is a list of wedding services with typical costs in UK sterling for both Italy and the UK. This list shows the cost of a typical wedding in the UK (arranged solely by the couple and with 100 guests) against the cost of a typical wedding in Italy (booked with a planner and with 30 guests).

Item	Italy Estimate (£)	UK Estimate (£)	Saving (£)	Your Quote	Actual Cost
Hairdressing & Make-up (inc. trial before the day)	65	50	- 15		
Flowers (posy & buttonhole)	0*	400	400		
Additional buttonholes (each)	7	7	0		
Corsage	8	8	0		
Transport	150	600	450		
Civil/Church Fees	0*	400	400		
Musicians at Ceremony	140	170	30		
DVD/Video of Ceremony	200	550	350		
Photography	400	850	450		
Reception venue hire	0*	650	650		
Reception food & drink (adults)	1600	4200	2600		
Wedding cake	0*	250	250		
Entertainment	300	300	0		
Favours and decorations	75	250	175		
Wedding Co-ordinator	660	0	- 660		
Total	**3605**	**8685**	**5080**		

*These items are usually included in the co-ordinator or tour operator fees, or in the "per head" cost of the wedding reception

Cost of all other items (typically purchased in the UK)

Item	Estimate (£)	Actual Cost
Flights for Bride & Groom	300	
Travel insurance	50	
Stationery & Postage	150	
Wedding ring (bride)	200	
Wedding ring (groom)	200	
Engagement ring	850	
Engagement gift	200	
Wedding dress	800	
Veil	175	
Attendants' outfits	500	
Suit hire (x5)	200	
Bride's accessories	125	
Skincare & make-up	250	
Hen & Stag parties	500	
Gifts for attendants & parents	250	
	4750	

Exchange Rates

Alright, this isn't the most scintillating of topics but believe me, it's relevant. You may not have thought this far ahead yet, but at some point it's going to become an issue.

Unlike UK suppliers, most suppliers in Italy will require deposits initially, and full payment before the date of the wedding. This is anathema to most UK couples (who only expect to pay things like full photography fees on receipt of the product), but in Italy it's normal practice to pay up front. In addition, most suppliers will ask you to pay in cash which will be an additional blow to those of you who were hoping to pay by credit card and spread the cost over a couple of interest-free months. This means that, in most situations, you will need to have the full cost of your wedding to hand before you tie the knot.

The cost of your wedding is quite likely to total over £1000, and of course the higher the total cost, the higher the bank charges associated with changing currency or transferring funds. Shopping for exchange rates takes on a whole new level of importance when you work out that a small difference in percentage can mean a saving of (sometimes) hundreds of pounds.

This brings us to the best way to pay suppliers. Unfortunately, unless you have a European bank account and store your funds in Euros, you won't be able to do a straight bank transfer or write a personal cheque. Cheques and transfers may be unavoidable when it comes to paying deposits (unless you can convince your supplier to accept something like Paypal), but with the cost of raising a foreign currency cheque at about £5 per item, you really want to keep these to a minimum. Before you start, shop around for the bank with the best looking fees for this service and, if necessary, open a wedding account there. A site such as www.moneysupermarket.com will be able to help you decide which account will be best suited.

When it comes to making final payments to your suppliers, the cheapest (if not the safest) way to go about it is to find the best exchange rate and change all your currency before you go. At time of writing, the best rates can be obtained through www.travelex.co.uk – order your currency online and pick it up from the airport when you depart (rather than exchanging at the airport where you will have to pay fees). If you decide to take this somewhat risky route, I'd advise spreading the cash out between various trusted guests to minimise the damage should any of it go astray. Travellers' cheques are, of course, much safer, but again you can pay quite high charges when it comes to cashing them in.

Insurance

I have to admit to being slightly sceptical when it comes to wedding insurance in general, but when it comes to weddings abroad I think it's something that's definitely worth budgeting for. The risk to the items you have to ship or carry with you is much higher, and if something goes missing or gets damaged you'll need to act quickly to replace the items without worrying about the extra cost. For a bit of extra peace of mind, the following companies provide insurance for weddings abroad:

www.weddingplaninsurance.co.uk
www.eandl.co.uk
www.mrlinsurance.co.uk

Country Information

"You might not be guaranteed good weather, but you've got a damn good chance!"
Lake Garda Bride

Average Climate Conditions

	Average Sunlight (hrs)	Average Temperature Min	Average Temperature Max	Heat & Humidity	Average precipitation (mm)	Wet days	Wedding Popularity
January	4	5	11	Low	71	8	Low
February	4	5	13	Low	62	9	Low
March	6	7	15	Low	57	8	Low
April	7	10	19	Low	51	6	Low
May	8	13	23	Moderate	46	5	Average
June	9	17	25	Medium	37	4	Very High
July	11	20	30	High	15	1	Very High
August	10	20	30	High	21	2	High
September	8	17	26	Moderate	63	5	Average
October	6	13	22	Low	99	8	Low
November	4	9	16	Low	129	11	Low
December	4	6	13	Low	93	10	Low

Source: Based on BBC Weather statistics for Rome

Public Holidays

January	1st – New Year's Day
	6th – Epiphany
March	Easter Weekend
April	(date depending on year)
	April 25th – Liberation Day, San Marco (Venice)
May	1st – Labour Day
June	2nd – Anniversary of the Republic
	24th – Saint John the Baptist (Turin, Genoa, Florence)
	29th – Sts Peter & Paul (Rome)
July	15th – Santa Rosalia (Palermo)
August	15th – Assumption of the Virgin
September	19th – San Gennaro (Naples)
October	4th – San Petronio (Bologna)
	30th – San Saturnio (Cagliari)
November	1st – All Saints' Day
	3rd – San Giusto (Trieste)
December	6th – Santa Nicola (Bari)
	7th – San Ambrose (Milan)
	8th – Day of the Immaculate Conception
	25th – Christmas Day
	26th – Boxing Day

Glossary

"Why does everyone keep shouting 'Augure!'?"

Sorrento Bride

This has been included not just to help you understand the words and phrases you'll hear bandied about, but also to assist you in any supplier searches you may want to carry out online.

Italian Sayings

Sposa bagnata, sposa fortunata
A wet bride is a lucky bride (i.e. rain is good!)

La buona moglie fa il buon marito
A good wife makes a good husband

Matrimoni e vescovati sono dal cielo destinati
Marriages are made in heaven

Il giorno piu bello della mia vita
The most beautiful day of my life

Il rito religioso in chiesa
The religious ceremony in church

Quello civile in comune
The civil ceremony in the town hall

Avrai una bella giornata
Have a wonderful day

Sposo novello
Newlywed

Evviva gli sposi / Augure
Congratulations to the Newly Weds

Appena Sposato
Just Married

Glossary

Baker	Fornaio
Bakery	Panetteria
Banns	Pubblicazione di matrimonio
Baptismal Certificate	Certificato di Battesimo
Barber	Parrucchiere per uomo / barbiere
Beautician	Estetista
Best wishes	Tanti auguri
Bride & Groom / Married Couple	Coppia di Sposi
Bridal Suite	Suite Matrimoniale
Bride	Sposa
Bride-to-be	Futura sposa / Fidanzata
Catering	Ricevimenti
Ceremony	Sposalizio
Certificate of No Impediment	Nulla Osta
Chapel	Cappella
Church wedding	Matrimonio in chiesa
Church	Chiesa
Civil wedding	Matrimonio civile
Confirmation Certificate	Certificato di Cresima
Congratulations	Congratulazioni
Favours (gift)	Bonboniere
Florist	Fioraio
Flower	Fiore
Flower arrangement	Composizione floreale
Flower basket	Cesto di fiori
Flower girl	Fioraia
Flower shop	Negozio di fiori
Get married	Sposarsi
Hairdresser / stylist	Parrucchiera / parruchiere
Honeymoon	Luna di miele

Husband	Marito
Husband & wife	Marito e moglie
Husband-to-be	Futuro marito
Lily	Fiore di giglio
Marriage office	Ufficio Matromonio
Marry	Sposare
My wife	Mia moglie
Photograph	Fotografia
Photograph album	Album fotografico
Photographer	Fotografo/a
Registrar	Ufficiale di Stato Civile
Registry office	Anagrafe
Town Hall	Comune / municipio
Wedded wife	Moglie Legittima
Wedding	Matrimonio / nozze
Wedding anniversary	Anniversario di matrimonio
Wedding attendant	Invitato
Wedding breakfast	Rinfresco nunziale
Wedding cake	Torta nunziale
Wedding clothes	Abiti nunziale
Wedding day	Giorno delle nozze
Wedding dinner	Pranzo di nozze
Wedding dress	Vestito da sposa
Wedding flower	Fiori nunziali
Wedding march	Marcia nunziali
Wedding party	Festa di matrimonio
Wedding ring	Fede nunziali
Wedding veil	Velo nunziale
Wife	Moglie

Essential Contacts

What follows are generic, country-wide contacts. Area-specific contacts and local suppliers are listed in the Area Guides.

For supplier searches, you can use online resources such as the Italian Yellow Pages, www.paginegialle.it/index.html, by entering the supplier type in "*Cosa*", and the location in "*Dove*". Remember to use the Italian town name, rather than the English translation.

Embassies & Consulate Offices

British Embassies in Italy
www.britishembassy.gov.uk
Tel: 06 4220 2220 (wedding information)

UK Foreign & Commonwealth Office
King Charles Street
London
SW1A 2AH
Tel: 020 7008 1500
www.fco.gov.uk

Italian Embassy in the UK
14 Three Kings Yard
London
W1K 4EH
Tel: 020 7312 2200
Fax: 020 7312 2230
ambasciata.londra@esteri.it
www.amblondra.esteri.it/Ambasciata_Londra

Italian Consulate General in London
38 Eaton Place
London
SW1X 8AN
Tel: 020 7235 9371
Fax: 020 7823 1609
consolato.londra@esteri.it
www.itconlond.org.uk

General Registrar of Births, Marriages & Deaths
Certificate Services Section
General Registrar Office, PO Box 2
Southport, PR8 2JD
Tel: 0845 603 7788
Fax: 01704 550013
certificate.services@ons.gsi.gov.ul

Overseas Section
General Registrar Office
Trafalgar Road
Southport, PR8 2HH
Tel: 0151 471 4801
Fax: 01633 652 988
overseas.gro@ons.gsi.gov.uk

www.gro.gov.uk

Irish Embassy in Italy
Piazza di Campitelli 3
00186 Rome
Tel: +39 06 697 9121
Fax: +39 06 697 2354
www.ambasciata-irlanda.it

Irish Department of Foreign Affairs
80 St. Stephen's Green
Dublin 2
Tel: +353 1 478 0822
Fax: +353 1 478 5951
http://foreignaffairs.gov.ie
marriageabroad@iveagh.gov.ie

Italian Embassy in Ireland
63/65 Northumberland Road
Ballsbridge
Dublin 4
Tel: 01 660 1744
Fax: 01 668 2759
Info@italianembassy.ie

US Embassies in Italy
www.usembassy.it

Italian Embassy in the US
3000 Whitehaven Street
NW – Washington
DC20008
Tel: 202 612 4400
Fax: 202 518 2154
www.ambwashingtondc.esteri.it

Italian Consulates in the US
www.italconsdetroit.org/statelocator/statelocator.htm

Marriage Offices / Uffici Matrimoni

Milan – Ufficio Anagrafe
Via Larga, 12
20122 Milano
Tel: +39 02 884 62132

Venice – Ca' Farsetti
San Marco, 4136
30124 Venezia
Tel: +39 04 1274 8833
Fax: +39 04 1274 8475

Genoa – Ufficio Matrimoni
Corso Torino, 11
16121 Genova
Tel: +39 010 557 6866
Fax: +39 010 541 720

Florence – Ufficio Stato Civile
Palazzo Vecchio,
Piazza Signoria
50100 Firenze
Tel: +39 055 276 8518
Fax: +39 055 261 6715

Rome – Ufficio Anagrafe
Via Petroselli, 50
00195 Roma
Tel: +39 06 671 03066

Naples – Ufficio Matrimoni
Piazza Municipio
Palazzo San Giacomo
80100 Napoli
Tel: +39 081 551 0364

Photographers / Fotografi (country-wide) – see the Area Guides for local suppliers

JoAnne Dunn Photographer
Via del Monte, 47b
84012 Angri
Salerno
Tel: +39 (0)81 947413
info@joannedunn.it
www.joannedunn.it

Ben Eden
5 Youngs Court
New End
Hampstead
London, NW3 1DD
Tel: +44 (0)207 084 4227
Fax: +44 (0)207 084 4279
ben@beneden.com
www.beneden.com

Italian Wedding Photographer
Info@italianweddingphotographer.com
www.italianweddingphotographer.com

Regency Wedding Photography
www.weddingsitaly.com/Photography

Wedding Co-ordinators / Agenzi per l'organizzazione delle nozze (country-wide)

The Book of Dreams
Tel: +39 081 532 12 23
info@thebookofdreams.net
www.thebookofdreams.net

By Cassini
90-100 Sydney Street
Chelsea
London
SW3 6NJ
Tel: +44 (0)790 387 9296
Tel: +39 347 799 3353
info@bycassini.com
www.bycassini.com

Destination Wedding Italy
www.destination-wedding-italy.com
info@destination-wedding-italy.com

Destination Weddings in Italy
www.destinationweddingsinitaly.com

Getting Married in Italy
Viale S. Lavagnini, 43
50129 Florence
Tel: +39 055 470443
Fax: +39 055 462 6657
info@gettingmarriedinitaly.com
www.gettingmarriedinitaly.com

Honeymoons and Weddings Abroad
Coopers Cottage
Portnoo Harbour
Portnoo
Donegal
ROI
Tel. 048 66 322 116
info@honeymoons-and-weddings-abroad.ie
www.honeymoons-and-weddings-abroad.ie

Italian Weddings
www.italian-weddings.com

Italy Weddings
info@italy-weddings.net
www.italy-weddings

Italy My Love
Tel: +39 349 583 4139
http://italymylove.com
info@italymylove.com

Matrimoniando
info@matrimoniando.it
www.matrimoniando.it

Weddings in Italy
www.weddingsinitaly.com

The Bridal Consultant
Unit 53
Moorgate Crofts Business Centre
Southgrove
Rotherham S60 2EN
Tel: 0845 9000 905
enquiries@thebridalconsultant.co.uk
www.thebridalconsultant.co.uk

Best Italian Weddings
III Settembre, 99
Dogana
RSM
Tel: +378 974 147
booking@bestitalianweddings.com
www.bestitalianweddings.com

Wedding Italy
Via de Gasperi, 6-8
33050 Gonars
Tel: +39 0432 931457
Fax: +39 0432 931196
mail@weddingitaly.com
www.weddingitaly.com

Weddings Abroad
Suite 8
Saville Exchange
Howard Street
North Shields
Tyne & Wear, NE30 1SE
Tel: +44 (0) 191 4066 228
info@weddingsabroad.com
www.weddingsabroad.com

Weddings Made in Italy
Tel: +44 (0)207 520 0470
Fax: +44 (0)207 278 4589
mail@weddingsmadeinitaly.co.uk
www.weddingsmadeinitaly.co.uk

Weddings In Italy
info@weddingsinitaly.it
www.weddingsinitaly.it

Romeo & Juliet Weddings
info@rj-weddings.com
www.romeoandjuliet-weddings.com

Exclusive Italy Weddings
Via Roma, 96
33033 Codroipo
Udine
Tel: +39 (0)432 913513
Fax: +39 (0)432 913809
info@exclusiveitalyweddings.com
www.exclusiveitalyweddings.com

Tour Operators / Agenti di Viaggi

Citalia
The Atrium
London Road
Crawley
West Sussex
RH10 9SR
Tel: 0870 901 4013
italy@citalia.co.uk
www.citalia.com

Cosmos
Dale House
Tiviot Dale
Stockport
Cheshire
SK1 1TB
Tel: 0870 44 35 285
cosmosairadmin@cosmos.co.uk
www.cosmos-holidays.co.uk

Cresta
Tel: 0870 238 7711
websales@bcttravelgroup.co.uk
www.crestaholidays.co.uk

First Choice
Tel: 0870 242 4247
www.firstchoice.co.uk

Kirker
4 Waterloo Court
10 Theed Street
London SE1 8ST
Tel: 0870 112 3333
Fax: 0870 066 0628
travel@kirkerholidays.com
www.kirkerholidays.com

Kuoni
Kuoni House
Dorking
Surrey DH5 4AZ
Tel: 01306 747007
holidays@kuoni.co.uk
www.kuoni.co.uk

Magic of Italy
Magic Weddings
King's Place
12-42 Wood Street
Kingston-upon-Thames
Surrey, KT1 1JF
Tel: 0870 888 0228
www.magicofitaly.co.uk

Thomas Cook
Tel: 0870 443 4582
www.thomascook.com
www.tcsignature.com

Thomson
Tel: 0870 608 0169
www.thomson.co.uk

Bibliography

Belford, Ros; Dunford, M; Woolfrey, C. *The Rough Guide to Italy*. London, England: Rough Guides, 2005.
Gillette-Browning, Christine. *Planning a Wedding*. London, England: Hodder & Stoughton, 1995
Granieri, Lori. *Abbondanza!* New York, USA: Citadel Press, 2002.
Podesta, Gina. *A Romantic's Guide to Italy*. Berkeley, Canada: Ten Speed Press, 2004.

Online Sources
http://foreignaffairs.gov.ie
www.ambasciata-irlanda.it
www.amblondra.esteri.it
www.ambwashingtondc.esteri.it
www.bbc.co.uk
www.britishembassy.gov.uk
www.clickbridal.com
www.comuni-italiani.it
www.confetti.co.uk
www.embitaly.org.uk
www.fco.gov.uk
www.fepqep.org
www.gro.gov.uk
www.hitched.co.uk
www.imdb.com
www.intoitaly.it
www.istat.it
www.italconsdetroit.org
www.italiansrus.com
www.italiantourism.com
www.italiantouristboard.co.uk
www.italyheaven.co.uk
www.italy-weddings.com
www.itconlond.org.uk
www.paginegialle.it
www.siafitalia.org
www.sposi.it
www.theknot.com
www.tripadvisor.co.uk
www.usembassy.it
www.virtualitalia.com
www.weddingchaos.co.uk
www.weddingguide.co.uk
www.weddings-abroad-guide.com
www.weddingsonline.ie
www.wordreference.com

Acknowledgements

I would like to thank the following people for their assistance in helping me put this work together: the staff at Positano Town Hall for help with legal information; Alessandra at The Book of Dreams for expert advice; Natalie from The Weddings Abroad Guide for general advice; Gina Podesta for general guidance (and Nancy Sayre for putting us in touch!); JoAnne Dunn and Camilla Cesarano for allowing me to use those wonderful photographs; Claire Gould, Joanna Kenrick, Louisa Heath and James Beard for editorial help and advice; all the tour operators who responded to my questionnaires, in particular Emma at Cresta Weddings and Joanne at Cosmos Weddings; all the (mainly) brides who responded to my questionnaires, in particular Clare Duvall, Lindsay Arnold, Becky Tisbury, Michelle Goodswen, Julie Jane, Edel Hunter and Lou; the message board participants of Hitched, Confetti, Wedding Guide, The Knot, The Weddings Abroad Guide and Weddings Online; all the brides who have bombarded me with emails to tell me about their frustrations and give me plenty of ideas, and all my friends for listening to me go on about this project for the last nine months.

I'd also like to thank my husband James, not only for marrying me in Italy in the first place but also for helping me with the research trips. Also thanks to my parents for doing a hell of a lot of unpaid leg work; you'll get a cut of the royalties, I promise.

Index

accessibility, **5**
accommodation, 5, 40, 41, 52
adoption certificate, 11, 12
affidavit of single status, **13**
age of consent, 9, 10, 11, 12
Amalfi, 14
Amalfi Coast, 2, 3, 6, 14, 35, 43
annulment, 12, 29
antipasti course, 36
apostille, 12
Archbishop, 29
Area Guides, 3, 4, 59
Arezzo, 14
atto notorio, 12, 49
auction (of the tie), 36
balances, 55
bands, 36
bank account, **54-55**
bank charges, **54-55**
bank transfers, **54-55**
banns, 13, 58
Baptismal Certificate, 29, 58
bellini, 35
Birth Certificate, 10, 11, 12, 29, 49
black, 34, 43
blessing, 26, 29, 30
bookings, 18, 19, 24, 49
bouquet, 33
Bravissimo, 45
bridal fashions, 43, 45
British Consulate, 10
British Embassy, 11, **60**, 66
British Nationals, 10
budget, 6, 16, 19, 24, 46, 48, **53-55**
budget planner, **53-54**
buses, 41
buttonholes, 53
canapés, 36
Capri, 14
carry-on luggage, 43, 55
cash. *See Currency*
Catholic Ceremonies, 26, **29-30**
Certificate of Freedom to Marry. *See Nulla Osta*
Certificate of No Impediment. *See Nulla Osta*
Certificates of Authority, 10
changing currency. *See Exchange Rates*
checklists, 3, **47-51**
cheques, 54
church, **29-30**, 33, 53, 57, 58
Church of England ceremonies, 30
civil ceremonies, 6, 21, **26-28**, 30, 57
Civil Registrar, 13
climate, 56
communication, **6**, 22
Communion Certificate, 29
Como, 14
comune. *See Town Hall*
confetti, 28, 32, 35
Confirmation Certificate, 29, 58
Consular District, 10, 11, **14**

consular officer, 12, 13
contacts, **59**
Convalidation. *See Blessing*
co-ordinator, 7, 8, 10, 13, 15, 17, 18, 20, **22-24**, 25, 26, 29, 30, 31, **63**
corno, 34
corsage, 53
courier, 23, 43
courses, 36
cousins, 9
currency, **54-55**
customs, 22, 25, **32-36**, 52
dancing, 36
deadlines. *See Checklists*
Death Certificate, 10, 11, 12
Decree Absolute. *See Divorce*
Deed Poll, 10, 11, 12
degrees of relationship, 9, 11
Department of Foreign Affairs, 11, **60**
deposits, 48, 54
dispensation, 11, 12, 13, 29, 30
divorce, 9, 10, 11, 12, 13, 29, 30
DIY planning, 15, 22, **25**
DJs, 36
documentation. *See Paperwork*
dress code, 41.
    see also Bridal Fashion, Suits, Suit Hire
drunkenness, 35
DVD, 53
Embassies & Consulate Offices, 25, **60**
entertainment, 36, 53
    See also Music
etiquette, **32-39**, 41
Euros. *See Currency*
exchange rates, **54-55**
exchanging of rings, 26, 27, 28, 30
fabric, 45
favours, **36**, 43, 53, 58
fees, 20, 24, 53, 54, 55
Ferrari, 2
Final Decree. *See Divorce*
final payments. *See Balances*
fish course, 36
flights, 5, 19, 37, 41, 43, **52**, 54
Florence, 14, 61
florist, 3, 15, 33, 49, 58
flowers, 16, 18, 45, 52, 53
Foreign & Commonwealth Office, **60**, 66
Form MP1, 12
Form MP2, 12
Form MP2B, 12
General Registrar Office, 14, **60**, 66
gift list, 41,
Giving Notice, 3, **9-10**, 48, 49, 50
glass, 36
gold, 34
Gospel, 29
green, 34
guest list, 37, 48, 50
hairdresser, 3, 15, 18, 58
hats, 43

Index

heat, 43, 45, 56
hold luggage, 43
Homily, 29
horn. See Corno
in-laws, 9-10, 33
insurance, 54, **55**
interpreter, 13, 20, 22, 26
Introductory Rites, 29
invitations, **37-39**, 49
Irish Embassy, 11, **60**
iron, 34
Ischia, 14
Italian Consulate, 60
Italian Embassy, 60
Italian sayings, 57
Italian traditions, 33-36
Jewish ceremonies, 30
kiss (the bride), 26, 36
Lake District, 6, 14
language. See Communication
Lecco, 14
legal requirements, 3, **8-13**, 18, 29
legalities, **7**, 22
lemon cream cake. See Wedding Cake
lilac, 34
Limoncello, 35
logistics, 43-45
low-cost airlines, 2, 5, 6, 43, **52**
Lucca, 14
luck, 34, 57
make-up, 45
marriage certificate, 10, 11, 12, **14**, 25,
marriage registration, 14
Mass. See Nuptial Mass
meat course, 36
menu, 16, 36
Milan, 14, 61
minimum stay requirements. See
  Residencey Requirements
mixed marriage, 29, 30
music, 26, 28, 36
Naples, 14, 61
notary, 11
Notice of Marriage, See Giving Notice
Nulla Osta, 10, 11, 12, 25
Nuptial Mass, 29-30
online resources, 52, 66
overhead locker, 43
package holidays, 17, 18, 19, 21
package weddings, 17
Padua, 14
paperwork, 6, 7, 8, 22, 23, 25, 28, 29, 30, 31
parents, 12
parish, 29, 30
passports, 10, 11, 12, 48, 49
pasta course, 36
Paypal, 54
photographer, 36, 43, 62
Pisa, 14
Positano, 14
practicalities, 6
pre cana, 29

pre-marital requirements, 30
Pretura, 12
previous marriage. See Divorce
priest, 29-30
private houses, 26
profiterole towers. See Wedding Cake
proof of marriage. See Marriage Certificate
prosecco, 35
Protestant ceremonies, 30
public holidays, 56
questionnaire, 11
rain, 34, 57
Ravello, 2, 14, 43
readings, 26, 28, 29
receiving lines, 35
reception, 3, 6, 19, **35-36**, 39
Registry Office, 10, 58
religious ceremonies, 6, 21, 26, **29-30**
renewal of vows, 31
residency requirements, 6, 18, 23,
risotto course, 36
Rite of Marriage, 30
road maps, 52
Rome, 2, 6, 11, 14, 61
rum baba. See Wedding Cake
same-sex partnerships, 31
sandles, 45
save-the-date cards, 37
school holidays, 5
shoes, 45
Siena, 14
signing of the register, 27, 29
solicitor, 11
Sorrento, 6, 14, 26, 43
special dispensation. See Dispensation
St Francesco Monastery Cloisters, 26
stationery, 37-39
  See also Invitations
statutory declaration, 12
step-relatives, 9
storage, 45
sugared almonds. See Confetti
suit carrier, 43
suit hire, 46
suits, 43, 46
Superintending Registrar, 10
superstitions, 34
suppliers, 18, 19, 22, 23, 24, 25, 59
sweat rash, 45
symbolic ceremonies, 30, 31
table plans, 52
tan lines, 45
tasks. See Checklists
teachers, 5
temperatures. See Heat
tie (auctioning of), 36
timescales. See Checklists
timings, 41
top table, 32, 36
tour operators, 6, **17-21**, 22, 25, 54, **65**
tourist season, 47

Index

Town Hall, 8, 10, 11, 12, 13, 14, 18, 23, 25, 26, 58
traditions, 22, 25, **32-36**
trains, 41, 52
transferring funds. *See Bank Transfers*
translations, 13, 14, 24, **57-58**
translator. *See Interpretor*
transportation, 33
travellers' cheques, 55
tribunale civile, 11, 12, 13
Tuscany, 14
typical costs. *See Budget Planner*
Ufficio Anagrafe, 58, **61**
Ufficio Matrimoni, 61
Ufficio Stato Civile, 13, 61
Umbria, 14
US Embassies, 13, 60
veil, 2, 44, 58
Veneto, 33
Venice, 6, 14, 35, 61

venue reviews, 3
Verona, 5, 14
Vespa, 2
video, 53
vows, 3, **27**, 30, 31
walking to the ceremony, 33
wedding account, 55
wedding cake, 15, 18, **35**, 36, 58
wedding certificate, 14, 25
wedding co-ordinators, 7, 8, 10, 13, 15, 18, **22-24**, 25, 26, 29, 30, 31, **63**
wedding dress, 43-45, 58
wedding information website, 40-41
Wedding Planner. *See Wedding Co-ordinator*
wedding planning sites, 52
wedding ring, 26, 28, 30
white ribbon, 34
witnesses, 11, 12, 25, 26, 49

Notes

Notes

Notes

Notes

Notes

Notes

Printed in the United Kingdom
by Lightning Source UK Ltd.
133466UK00001B/376/A